Acclaim for Robert Raines and *To Kiss the Joy*

From his first book, Robert Raines has written in beauty and poetry of his pilgrimage of faith. Again he pens a book that helps one to experience life with him.—*The Disciple*

You have been needing to talk to someone? Then simply sit down with this book and discuss your problem and need with Dr. Raines. He answers personally and with great sensitivity the questions which are on your heart.—Velma S. Daniels, *News Chief*

. . . one of those delightful personal books, possibly described as devotional, wherein the author talks about recognizing difficulties, developing confidence and moving on to dependence upon God.—*Baptist Standard*

To Kiss the Joy is fresh, vital, pulsing with Christian faith. . . . A stimulating, inspiring book, one to be treasured and shared.—*Religion in the News*

Fourteen highly readable essays. . . . The author leads one carefully into spiritual handling of life's pains and joys.—*Christianity Today*

There is a gentleness and sincerity which permeates the book, attracting the reader's interest and holding it firmly to the last page. . . . One of the finer books about religion . . . low-keyed, honest and most important, sets out in precise terms how believing in God ultimately translates into believing in yourself.—*Pyramid Books*

[*To Kiss the Joy*] is like an intimate conversation with a caring friend.—*The Columbus Enquirer*

To Kiss The Joy

ROBERT A. RAINES

Abingdon Press
Nashville

TO KISS THE JOY

A Festival Book

Copyright © 1973 by Word, Incorporated
Waco, Texas 76703

All rights reserved

Festival edition published by Abingdon Press,
October 1983

ISBN 0-687-42185-3 (originally published by
Word Books under ISBN 0-87680-324-9)

Printed in the United States of America

This little book is dedicated to all those people who have helped me grow in my own humanity, and especially those at First Community Church.

The essays herein are not developmental, but are more like spokes of a wheel that have to do with my own experiences of personal struggle and growth and discovery in recent years, and the experiences of those people I have been privileged to know. Let each one stand by itself, and each one be a handle you may use in a way that is appropriate and right for you.

I think that growth is less a linear matter of starting in the valley and climbing ever further up the mountain, and more a matter of exploring the terrain in which there will be mountains and valleys and fields and rivers and streams. One doesn't get better and better, but simply learns more and perhaps grows in human understanding and in the capacity, without compromising one's own vision, to understand and accept people in the reality of their failings, their mistakes, their ecstasies, their tragedies—and to understand in a little more depth how amazing the grace of God must be to accept us all as we are.

Robert A. Raines

October, 1973

CONTENTS

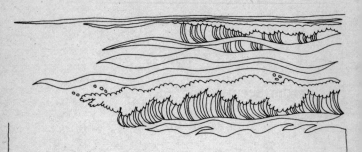

From
Security to Trust

SOME TIME ago, walking along a sandy beach, I came across a crab who skittered sideways away from me, afraid of my strange intrusion into his sand and sea world. I watched his erratic errands across the sand and among the rocks with the waters rushing in, as they have been rushing in there for hundreds of millions of years, long before there was any human eye to see the water or hear its roar. I pondered the probability of another time in the distant future when those waves or their successors will roll in and the descendant of that crab will be skittering sideways there—when once again there will be no human eye to notice or ponder, and the human experiment is over.

I thought about the fate of men and crabs. I remembered that a crab in order to live and grow must from time to time discard its shell with its familiar creature comforts, that until it succeeds in creating a new shell, it is extremely vulnerable. Its life story is a passage through successive shells until one day it succeeds too well and makes a shell so strong and rigid that it can't escape from it. That is the shell in which it dies.

You and I, too, live under the shelter of shells—belief systems, moral codes, life styles which provide security for us. When those shells crack or break into pieces, we, too, are left skittering sideways on some windswept beach, vulnerable until we can create new belief systems, new moral directives. We suffer in this time the cracking of ancient theological and ethical shells. Some of the old landmarks and guideposts are gone. We don't have any new ones yet, so we are vulnerable —in between the shells—in between the times.

Johnny Mercer warned us years ago about such a condition in a popular song. Remember his philosophy: "Ac-cent-tchu-ate the positive, e-lim-my-nate the negative. . . . Don't mess with Mister In-Between." But that is where we now are —in between, coming out of one time in our lives, but not yet into another time—in between the times, on the way in the wilderness, vulnerable, like the people of Israel in the desert.

It is easy to condemn those people for making a golden calf, but we should understand that they, too, were in between the times. They were feeling vulnerable, out of Egypt, and not yet into the Promised Land. And where was Moses, anyway, and his strange God who put them into this awful situation? Sometimes they wanted to go back to the dependable safety of slavery, afraid of the unknown risks ahead, afraid they wouldn't survive. Like us, they wanted to curl up in front of some fire against the cold unknown, snuggle under the covers, those security blankets which shelter us against our vulnerability and protect us against the terrible freedom to decide. So they made a golden calf! Something tangible, something that they could see and look at and touch. You can depend on a golden calf. There it is. Something to worship.

A golden calf is any security system we make to protect us against the strange God of Moses who intrudes on our sand and sea world, with that terrible risk of being responsible for our lives. I want to explore two of these golden calves and suggest how we may move from needing that kind of security to being ready for a different kind of trust.

First, we can move from security in our beliefs to trust in God. We all want to be secure in our beliefs, to feel safe in the universe, comfortable with God, to get relief from that awful sense of contingency that sometimes comes upon us in the night. In this very anxious time in which we live, there has been a marked resurgence in many forms of the human search for security. There is the rapid growth of fundamentalist religion strikingly evident on the college campus today. Fundamental religion offers *the* truth, *the* way, unconditional security as lure and reward. And then there is the wide curiosity in astrology, tarot cards, the occult, any dependable determinism which can relieve us of the burden of deciding for ourselves and taking responsibility for our lives—the kind of determinism that takes away our freedom and gives us instead a fake-filled security.

Or there is the yearning among many of us who are older for the comfort of the Church in the Wildwood, the Little Brown Church in the Vale, a Currier and Ives time when God was in his heaven and all was right with the world. "Those were the days," as Archie and Edith Bunker sing. Or there is the frantic attempt of some of us who are younger to latch onto the newest idea, that new experience, that new product, that new group, that promises to make us safe and secure from all alarms in three easy lessons or six brief meetings for $10.95. We all need security, and we all search for it.

What golden calf of security glitters for you?

All of our attempts to make ourselves secure are expressions of the deep cry from every one of us calling into the void, "Do you love me? Do you love me?" We all need some security. Few of us can live creatively for very long in a state of vulnerability. One mark of health is a minimum need for security and the capacity to cope when one's particular shell breaks. I remember a sermon by a seminary professor entitled "Don't Knock Out the Bridge" in which he warned seminary students against storming into congregations and destroying people's faith systems without helping them build new bridges of faith. Walk on whatever bridges are still able to support you. Remember that bridges of faith—like most human constructs when the pressure gets bad—crumple and fade out, break into pieces. So don't be surprised if times come when you find yourself in between bridges, shells, in between the times, vulnerable.

How are your bridges holding up these days? Do you feel that you are skittering sideways along the beach of your lifeline in some way? In his book *After Auschwitz*, Richard Rubenstein, a rabbi, confessed that he could no longer believe in a God who was supposed to be protecting his chosen people, because he had not done so in that terrible experience.[1] Reading what he had to say made me realize that for some time I had not been believing in a God who *controls* history because, if so, a lot of awful things have to be laid at his door. Our own little Auschwitz experiences, our little tragedies, which are not little to us and which shatter our own comfortable shells, may leave us with a radical kind of questioning. For me, this questioning began some time ago. It has not ended, and I don't suppose it will.

How does God work within history if he doesn't *control* it? How does God work his purpose within our lives? How is our prayer efficacious? What meaning is there in our tragedies and finally in our death? For me, answers to those questions and others like them, even biblical answers, don't quite satisfy my appetite to understand, my longing to know. I suspect there may be no answers for us, as there were no answers for Job, apart from our own personal encounters with God where, from within, we may discover that it is possible to trust him in the dark without evidence.

Being human, we have to keep trying to construct answers. We have to try to understand even though we know that our answers are partial and ephemeral. Loren Eiseley helps me. He says, "It is not sufficient any longer to listen at the end of the wire to the rustlings of galaxies; it is not enough even to examine the great coil of DNA in which is coded the very alphabet of life. . . . But beyond lies the great darkness of the ultimate Dreamer who dreamed the light and the galaxies. Before act was, or substance existed, imagination grew in the dark." [2] O to be able to trust God—to let your imagination grow in the dark of your own experience and maybe to meet the Dreamer from time to time in your own deeps! Someone put it this way, "When all human props fail and all the bridges are out and there is nothing to hang onto any longer, then deep down in me there is something." Something! Something that makes life possible; something that starts me building another bridge; something that calls for a faith without evidence; something in you and me.

As for me, over the years one belief or doctrine after another has been shaken or shed. And each time I felt my faith threatened only to discover that deeper down at another level there was a place where I could stand. Today I feel less need of security in beliefs, in the human constructs by which we attempt to interpret our experiences. Because, in a small way, I feel free to trust in God. Perhaps I have not been very severely tested, but I do feel the confidence of Paul that nothing in creation—nothing I can do; nothing that can be done to me; even nothing that can happen to those who are most precious to me—*nothing* can separate me or you from God's love which is in you, me, and the trees and the crabs, and which comes clear in Jesus.

I believe that God's love for you and me is unconditional. His word comes to us in the words of the hymn, "That soul, though all hell should endeavor to shake, I'll never, no, never, no, never forsake." That's not a lot to believe, but there is someone to trust. As James Pike put it, "We need fewer beliefs, and more belief."

And when we are free of the need to be secure in beliefs, then we are ready for the wilderness journey. Such a journey is described in the story of the Bedouin guide who led a traveler over a mountain pass after a night spent in an oasis in the valley now far below them. As he stopped his mount at the top of the track, he contemplated for a long moment and then looked out at the new vista of sand wastes that had just opened ahead of them. Inhaling deeply the pure, dry, clean, empty and odorless wind of the desert, he said, "Can you still smell the exquisite fragrance of the orchards behind us? Its headiness is that of wine and its warmth a woman's. But do you now smell the wind of the wilderness? It is the breath of God." [3] We can move from security in our beliefs to trust in God.

And second, we can move from security in being right to

trust in God. We all want to be secure in being right. We don't want to make mistakes. We want to be the good guys. So we devise ethical systems, moral conventions and life styles to which we can conform and try to get everybody else to conform, even to the smallest items of clothes and hair, the movies we are supposed to like, the cars we drive, the houses we live in, and so on and so on. We try to make a neat and tidy distinction between what is right and what is wrong, what is good and what is bad. We believe that if we can stick with what is good and right, then we can legitimately feel that we are right, even that we are righteous, even that we are free to condemn those who don't buy our particular style! So, unwittingly, we become carbon copies of the spiritual climate of our environment, secure in the certainty that we are right, conforming to whatever is the convention in which we live and move. Our conformity is a way of saying to our neighbors near and far, "Now, look, I am doing what you think I ought to do. I am living the way you think I ought to live. Do you love me? Do you love me?"

But in truth we can have no assurance that we are right. Our decisions are made not in the context of certainty but of ambiguity. *The Cruel Sea*, a novel of the Second World War, is a striking illustration of ambiguities with which many of us could identify. A convoy is on its way across the Atlantic. A German U-boat is loose in the convoy. It has already hit and sunk several ships. There are scores of survivors screaming in the oily waters for help. A destroyer escort to the convoy suddenly gets a blip on its sonar which is the U-boat. The destroyer steers on a course which will take it directly over the U-boat to depth bomb it. The captain prepares to give the order to drop that bomb, only to see a few yards ahead of where his destroyer is going dozens of these people in the water screaming for help. In a second he has to decide whether to plough ahead, killing the people in the water but hoping to get the U-boat—only hoping, no guarantee, to get that U-boat and to save the rest of the convoy—or veer off, saving those people but losing the U-boat, maybe never to get it into range again, and so to jeopardize the whole convoy. He decides to plough ahead, kills those people, and gets that U-boat.

There is no pure decision. Most decisions that you and I make as individuals, as a family, at work, in the community, are made in the context of ambiguity. Whatever option we choose from those available to us will help someone and hurt someone else. We are to love our neighbors. It is easy to reduce the Ten Commandments and all the others to one—Love —which infinitely simplifies and infinitely complicates it. Because it means that in a given situation, each of us has to try to determine what is the most loving action for all the neighbors involved. The more important the decision, the more ambiguous the circumstances, and the more uncertain and unpredictable the consequences. We can seldom have any certainty that we make a right decision. There may be no right decisions. There may be only options where we are responsible to choose.

I used to labor under a particular kind of burden. I used to feel that in any given context and among all the options available, one of them was God's will. And, by God, I had to find it so I wouldn't make an awful mistake and have to feel that terrible guilt of having missed it. Well, I don't feel that way any more. In any given context, among the options available, I believe that we are responsible to try to seek what love would indicate with the persons and groups involved. We are responsible to weigh consequences, to assess probabilities, to take what seems to be the most loving and wise course of action. And then, as always, to trust that whatever we decide, however we choose, even if it is wrong, even if the consequences are disastrous, even if the choice is foolish or malicious—even so, God stays with us to forgive us and help pick up the pieces, build another bridge, try all over again. Martin Luther's comment is comforting to me, "Trust God and sin on bravely."

We cannot avoid participating in evil insofar as evil consists of making decisions that either hurt, in part, or fail to help, in part, some other person or persons. We cannot be perfect. We do not need to be. We should not try to be. What a relief it is not to have to be right! Not least because when you know you are right, then you have the awful obligation of having to set everybody else right! You've got no time off for your own enjoyment.

We are not called to be right but to be responsible, to make the best choice we can in a given circumstance, and to trust that God will bring something creative out of what happens. We no longer need the security of our beliefs or the security of being right when we are able to trust in God. Our search for security, our making of a golden calf, is our way of asking God and each other, "Do you love me?"

James Baldwin describes an incident which expresses our longing for love and security:

The joint, as Fats Waller would have said, was jumping. . . . And, during the last set, the saxophone player took off on a terrific solo. He was a kid from some insane place like Jersey City, or Syracuse, but somewhere along the line he had discovered that he could say it with a saxophone. He stood there, wide-legged, humping the air, filling his barrel chest, shivering in the rags of his twenty-odd years, and screaming through the horn, "Do you love me?" "Do you love me?" . . . the same phrase unbearably, endlessly, and variously repeated with all the force the kid had. . . . The question was terrible and real. The boy was blowing with his lungs and guts out of his own short past; and somewhere in the past, in gutters or gang fights . . . in the acrid room, behind marijuana or the needles, under the smell in the precinct basement, he had received a blow from which he would never recover, and this no one wanted to believe. Do you love me? Do you love me? The men on the stand stayed with him cool and at a little distance, adding and questioning. . . . But each man knew that the boy was blowing for every one of them. . . .[4]

Can you smell the wind of the wilderness? It is the breath of God, whispering to you and me, "I love you, I love you, I love you."

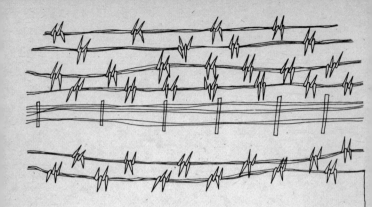

The
Dynamics of Growth

ALEXANDER Solzhenitsyn, in his novel *The First Circle*, describes life in an elite Russian prison camp at the end of World War II. At one point in the book, two men are talking. Sologdin, middle-aged, has already spent twelve years in this prison. Endless years stretch ahead of him. He has lost his wife, his children, property—all but his life. Yet, strangely, the experience has not embittered him nor destroyed his spirit, but rather distilled his humanity to a deep, rare wisdom.

Nerzhin is the second man—a brilliant young scientist in his early years of imprisonment. He seeks out the older man for insight into his own years of deprivation stretching ahead of him.

Sologdin looked past Nerzhin into the zone, at the thick little clumps of bushes all furry with frost and just touched by the gentle pink of the east. The sun seemed uncertain whether to show itself or not. Sologdin's face, drawn and lean, with his reddish-grey, curly little beard and his short mustache, revealed some ancient Russian quality. . . .

"How to face difficulties?" he declared again. "In the realm of the unknown, difficulties must be viewed as a *hidden treasure!* Usually, the more difficult, the better. It's not as valuable if your difficulties stem from your own inner struggle. But when difficulties arise out of increasing objective resistance, that's *marvelous!* " [1]

Sologdin continues:

"Failures must be considered the cue for further application of effort and concentration of will power. And if substantial efforts have already been made, the failures are all the more joyous. It means that our crowbar has struck the iron box containing the treasure. Overcoming the increased difficulties is all the more valuable because in failure the *growth of the person performing the task* takes place in proportion to the difficulty encountered!" [2]

As I saw that prison, its pygmy-souled authorities with the power of life and death over a giant-souled man like Sologdin, I realized with a new clarity that position, power, status, prestige, authority, success are finally not what matter at all. What could Sologdin have of any of these things? What matters is not success or failure but *growth*, the growth of the human being. That's what is left when it's all over, when it's just beginning.

What matters for you and for me in our various prisons of age, health, family, sex, job, circumstances—all that limits us and confines us—what matters is not success or failure in any quantitative sense, but *growth*. Not what we are by reason of external achievement, but who we are becoming in terms of the humanity growing within us. What prison am I in? What prison are you in? What is now binding us, restricting, confining, restraining us?

This powerful novel of a man's humanity growing like a flower out of a rock, in the midst of grotesque inhumanities, laid bare for me the dynamics of growth. There are two such dynamics. The first dynamic of growth is *recognition*. Growth begins when we recognize that difficulties are opportunities to grow, that failure is an open door to the future, that the iron box of frustration contains treasures of insight and strength.

Paul put all of this recognition in religious terminology when he wrote:

> But we have this treasure in earthen vessels, to show that the transcendent power belongs to God and not to us. We are afflicted in every way, but not crushed; perplexed, but not driven to despair; persecuted, but not forsaken; struck down, but not destroyed; always carrying in the body the death of Jesus, so that the life of Jesus may also be manifested in our bodies.[3]

Paul encourages us to recognize, at the heart of our death-dealing experiences, the life-giving power of God. Not that God sends difficulties upon us, but that he is hidden in them as the power to endure, to overcome, to grow. Growth begins when we recognize God in our difficulties.

But so often we're blind and deaf to God's presence in our difficulties because of our own pain or anger, resentment, self-pity. We indulge in what may be called the "if only" syndrome. If only I had another job, if only my boss would move or be transferred or have a heart attack, if only I could make another five or ten thousand a year. If only I weren't short and pimply-faced, or tall and awkward, or successful and empty. If only my parents would listen to me. If only my kids would do what I tell them to do. If only I didn't have allergy, nervous colon, omnipresent in-laws, a house decaying under my feet and teeth decaying in my mouth. If only, if only, if only. Growth begins when we stop saying "if only" and start to recognize that difficulties are opportunities to grow.

Some time ago at the board meeting of an ecumenical organization, there was an impasse. The diversity on that board was impressive. There were real blacks, real Jews, real Catholics, real Protestants, real conservatives, real radicals. Over the years in the pressure cooker of that community, I learned something of my own WASPishness—how I see things, the world and other people, through white, educated, privileged, Protestant lenses. I kid myself if I think I see through clear, human lenses. I don't and you don't. Nobody does. Everybody sees through the particular lenses of his own limited experiences. That's why the majority can never understand why a minority doesn't want to be integrated, forgetting that for a minority, integration—whether it's racial or national or religious—usually means assimilation, the obliteration of particularities.

The idea of a melting pot is really misleading because, finally, Jews and blacks and other minorities do not want to melt into a white Christian pot. We are discovering in our time the validity of a pluralistic society where real differences in behavior, in life style, in dress, in perspective, in value systems are acknowledged, respected and confirmed.

At that board meeting, we wrestled with these significant differences, and we could not reconcile them. I felt that night an urgent need somehow to break through that impasse so that things would start flowing and growing again together—somehow to break the log jam. The nation today needs to break through an impasse. Congregations need to, and people who work together need to. Families need to.

Some time ago our family came to an impasse on many matters. So we had a leveling session in which we talked over bedtime hours, allowances, who's supposed to wash the dishes when, baby-sitting, TV on school nights, and so on. It was loud and it was hectic, but things began flowing and we began growing together again. Anger and frustration were ventilated, and for awhile Nancy did the laundry on time, Barbie picked up Nancy at ballet without complaining; and Peg and I were able once again to affirm all the wonderful things about them that are there. Growth begins, then, when we recognize difficulties as opportunities to grow. Growth begins when we recognize failure as an open door to the future.

Not long ago I was working on a project with a friend. He wrote me a letter which shocked and scared me. He said that it seemed to him, as we had worked together, that I was uncomfortable when the leadership was not in my hands, when I wasn't in control. Therefore, he said, I tended to use people to get my purpose accomplished rather than coöperate to produce a mutual result. I was shocked because I hadn't been aware that my friend thought I was trying to control him, nor was I aware of his anger about the matter. And I was scared because I hadn't been aware myself that I was trying to control him. Evidently there was some distance between my image of myself and the real me.

We met for lunch and talked together, and that day I learned something valuable about myself and grew a little in my humanity. That particular failure of mine was an open door to a more honest, more profound friendship with this man in the future. Failure is the greatest teacher of all. It strips away illusions that will go by no other process. It makes us realize that something doesn't work. It forces us to try new approaches, to think new thoughts; it breaks us loose of the blocks, the prison, the routine, the habits, the rigidities that we just get sucked into and held within. When we face up to a failure, we discover resources within us that enable us to learn, to overcome, to grow. Growth begins when we recognize failure as an open door to the future, when we recognize that the iron box of frustration contains treasures of insight and strength.

Whenever you have an enforced period of confinement or immobility, when you're sick or, for whatever reason, have a lot of time alone by yourself, you have a chance to think, to cultivate your own depths, a chance to keep company with your own soul. It can be a very healing, quieting time. It can also be a very threatening time because sometimes we're afraid to be alone with ourselves.

People in hospitals and nursing homes, people who live alone, know about this kind of solitude. Prisoners know about it. So did this brilliant young scientist, Nerzhin. Of him it was said that "because of his intense inner life, [he] was free of envy." [4] I'm intrigued by that. I've pondered it. I'd like to be free of envy. Wouldn't you?

How do you develop an intense inner life? Prayer is the anguished longing to grow in difficulties; prayer is the patience born of unfulfilled hopes. Prayer is appropriating the fruits of failure. Prayer is believing that there is treasure in every iron box. Prayer is courage to keep on searching for it, confidence that at the rock bottom of everything, every event and every person, is God. Prayer is taking time to remember all that, and hope it, and keep on hoping it. Growth begins, then, when we recognize God at the heart of our difficulties. Growth continues when we respond to God in our difficulties.

The second dynamic of growth is *response*. Sologdin continues speaking to the young man, Nerzhin, saying:

> "And now listen: The rule of the Final Inch! The realm of the Final Inch! . . . The work has been almost completed, the goal almost attained. . . . But the quality of the thing is not *quite* right. . . . In that moment of fatigue and self-satisfaction it is especially tempting to leave the work without having attained the apex of quality. . . . In fact, the rule of the Final Inch consists in this: not to shirk this crucial work. Not to postpone it. . . . And not to mind the time spent on it, knowing that one's purpose lies not in completing things faster but in the attainment of perfection." [5]

Growth continues, then, when we wrestle difficulties into opportunities, wring success out of failure, crack open that iron box and get the treasure. Paul puts this in religious terminology when he writes:

> . . . We do not lose heart! Though our outward humanity is in decay, yet day by day we are inwardly renewed. . . . Our eyes are fixed, not on the things that are seen, but on the things that are unseen . . . [6]

Growth continues when we respond to God in our difficulties, when we decide, when we choose, when we act, when we say yes or no.

Sometimes we respond to God by taking negative action, deciding not to do something, saying no to a sure thing. Gay Talese, in his book about the *New York Times, The Kingdom and the Power,* tells a marvelous story about Adolph Ochs, publisher of the *Times* in the 1920s. He says:

Ochs had an instinct for avoiding the temptations of business.... [At one time] he was so short of money that, to save
a few pennies, he would sometimes wander through *The
Times* shutting off the lights over desks not in use—and *yet*,
when a prominent New Yorker, a trusted friend, offered him
a contract for $150,000 worth of municipal advertising with
no strings attached, Ochs refused. He did so on the theory
that he needed the revenue so desperately that he might ad-
just his operation to the windfall and he was unwilling to
trust himself as to what he might do if, after that had happened, he was threatened with a cancellation of the contract.
Ochs was a very human man with his share of human frail-
ties and, knowing this, he was wary of the slightest twitch
of temptation in himself.[7]

I would be as careful of the integrity of my humanity as
Ochs was of the integrity of his newspaper. Don't you ad-
mire that exercise of the will power in the realm of the Final
Inch?

Today we do not know how not to have everything. We
know little about self-denial, even less about discipline. Yet,
it is doubtful if major achievement in any field, especially that
of growing to our full human potential, can be accomplished
without discipline, without pain, without self-denial, of one
sort or another. The ability to say no to ourselves today for
the sake of some better tomorrow, the capacity to postpone
present gratification for future fulfillment, the courage to
make choices and abide by them, to know our own weaknesses, to anticipate them, not to allow them to reign over
us, not to let the glorious idea of doing your own thing be
carte blanche to do anything—such ability to say no is critical
to growth. We may not be captains of our souls, but neither
are we slaves of our circumstances or our psyches. We are
responsible for who we are becoming! Is there some sure thing
in our lives now to which we should say no?

Sometimes we respond to God by taking positive action, deciding to do something, saying yes to a wild possibility. Svetlana, Stalin's daughter, while in India chanced to read Chester Bowles's book, *Ambassador's Report*, and was struck by this passage: "It is possible for a single individual to defy the whole might of an unjust empire to save his honor, his religion, his soul, and lay the foundation for that empire's fall or its regeneration." [8] With those words burning into her being, on the spur of the moment she called a taxi and had the driver take her from the Soviet section of town to the United States embassy, where she asked for asylum. In a moment, all the frustration and longing of her forty years were lanced by those words, and she decided to leave the old life behind for a daring leap into the unknown future.

So, you and I can lay the foundation for the renewal of a family, a congregation, a nation, our own life, by one courageous action. The realm of the Final Inch may call for us to look for things unseen, to jump over a fence, to change a job, to do a new thing, to think a new thought, to be radically open now, in the present, to the Spirit of God who is alive.

We are in charge of our lives. We can do great things! John Gardner says one of the reasons mature people stop learning is that they become less and less willing to risk failure. But without great risks there can be no great rewards! We can't ooze into the future. We have to leap into it. Sometimes we grow literally by leaps and bounds. Sometimes our pygmy selves grow into giant selves by taking one small step of hope.

Is there some small step of hope just waiting to be taken? Is there some wild possibility before us now to which we really want to say yes?

Strength in
Our Weakness

A FEW years ago a job possibility came my way that really turned me on. I got the itch for that job. Over a period of a year a lot of candidates were looked over, and at the end of the year three of us were left. By that time, I could taste that job, and it tasted good! So I waited for a week, a couple of weeks, a month, six weeks—for a phone call that never came. Then one day I got a "Dear Mr. Raines" letter which informed me that another man had been chosen. I felt tremendous disappointment and devastation. It was one of the first times in my life that I had wanted something badly and couldn't have it. And there was nothing that I could do about it. A door was slammed shut on me and I was powerless to open it. I experienced my powerlessness to control my own future.

In the months that followed, I struggled to cope with what

I felt as personal rejection. For awhile I withdrew into a quietness which was unusual for me, licking my wounds, pretending that I didn't really care that much about it, too proud to admit how much it hurt. But my friends knew anyway. Then there were moments of ego defense when I thought to myself, "Those idiots, they could have had me, and they chose that other guy. They deserve what they're not going to get!" Then onslaughts of self-pity, "Oh, what might have been," and a gnawing ache and pain somewhere in my chest that didn't go away for more than a year.

Slowly, over those months, I began to learn a little about the limitations of my life, the intractability of events and circumstances that strip us of our power to control our own future, that whittle us down to our essential humanity and make us vulnerable. In that period, out of the soil of humiliation, a tiny, tiny seed of humility began to grow.

Perhaps you too have experienced your powerlessness to control your future.

Maybe you lose your job. The weeks and months go by and nothing right comes along, and the devastation and the fear and self-doubts set in, and you learn about powerlessness to control your own future. Or maybe your marriage breaks up. You go through the anguish of divorce or rejection, then start out all over alone, without any guarantees of anything, and it is frightening. And, of course, whenever a serious question mark is stamped on our health or the health of a loved one, suddenly we realize that we and those precious to us live by a slender thread that can snap in a moment.

Maybe you experience the terror of making it big. You arrive at the top and you look over from the top only to discover that the view isn't any different. You've arrived—but where? There is an emptiness. You've made it, but what is it you've made—and who are you anyhow? Is this all there is?

The forms of the experience of powerlessness are many and varied. Whenever there is a threat to the strength on which we've counted without even thinking about it—our virility, our beauty, our ability to support our family and to cope with our emotional problems—whenever that happens, we find ourselves undermined where we thought we were invulnerable. Backed into a corner, shaking and trembling, struggling to stay on our feet and not to go to pieces or dissolve into self-pity, or on the other hand to grow hard, bitter, cynical, closed up, tight—how do we stay open, warm, suffering, vulnerable, hoping?

The people of Israel felt like that in exile—powerless to get free, their chosen future cut off. So they cried out with words to which you and I are not strangers: "My way is hid from the Lord, and my right is disregarded by my God." [1] He's forgotten about me; he doesn't see what is happening to me, or if he does, he's not doing anything about it, and maybe he can't do anything about it. That's the worst—maybe he can't.

So to the people in their time of powerlessness, the young man Isaiah spoke words which may also be a word of the Lord to you and me in our time of powerlessness:

> Have you not known? Have you not heard?
> The Lord is the everlasting God,
>   the Creator of the ends of the earth.
> He does not faint or grow weary,
>   his understanding is unsearchable.
> He gives power to the faint,
>   and to him who has no might he increases strength.
> Even youths shall faint and be weary,
>   and young men shall fall exhausted;
> but they who wait for the Lord shall renew their strength,
>   they shall mount up with wings like eagles,

they shall run and not be weary,
they shall walk and not faint. [2]

It's only when you *have to* that you get interested in what it might mean to wait for the Lord. Waiting is a matter of letting it happen to you rather than doing it to somebody else. It's a matter of being receptive rather than aggressive, of making ready rather than taking action, of letting yourself be vulnerable rather than protecting and defending.

I'd like to make three suggestions as to how the Lord renews our strength when we are willing and able to wait for it. The first is this: *the Lord renews our strength to be patient.*

King Lear is a very impatient man. In his eighties he prepares to divest himself of his power and give it to his three daughters. Then he makes the gross mistake of asking them, "Which of you shall we say doth love us most?"—a mistake that you and I sometimes make when we ask for a command performance from children or colleagues.

Regan and Goneril, who despise their father, pretend great love for him. Cordelia, who loves her father, is silent. Lear, who "slenderly" knows himself, does not understand that sometimes love is silent. So in a rash moment of impetuous anger, he disinherits Cordelia, who loves him, and bequeaths his power to Regan and Goneril, who despise him. Step by step through the play, these two "tiger daughters" humiliate their father, reduce his rights and privileges, until finally Lear realizes that they are bound and determined to reduce him to absolute powerlessness. He, Lear the King, cries out in anguished, unbelieving rage:

You heavens, give me that patience, patience I need!
You see me here, you gods, a poor old man,
As full of grief as age; wretched in both!

[34]

> If it be you that stir these daughters' hearts
> Against their father, fool me not so much
> To bear it tamely; touch me with noble anger,
> And let not women's weapons, water-drops,
> Stain my man's cheeks! No, you unnatural hags,
> I will have such revenges on you both
> That all the world shall—I will do such things,—
> What they are yet I know not,—but they shall be
> The terrors of the earth. . . . [3]

Lear, who in his power needed no patience, discovers in his powerlessness his need to be patient. Through the play, Lear's suffering is a kind of crucifixion that drives him nearly to madness. He comes into a new birth of understanding and compassion for the weak for whom he has previously had contempt. He sees himself and his daughters as they are. He meets Cordelia in prison. As he kneels before her—he, the King, before the daughter, his subject—he says: "I am a very foolish fond old man. . . . Pray you now, forget and forgive. . . ." [4] And then in a burst of newborn joy, he says to her:

> We two alone will sing like birds i' the cage:
> When thou dost ask me blessing, I'll kneel down,
> And ask of thee forgiveness: so we'll live,
> And pray, and sing, and tell old tales, and laugh
> at gilded butterflies, and hear poor rogues
> Talk of court news; and we'll talk with them too,
> Who loses and who wins; who's in, who's out;
> And take upon's the mystery of things,
> As if we were God's spies . . . [5]

Lear is every inch a king when he has lost his kingdom and found himself, his own humanity. It is only in his powerlessness that he learns who he is and who his daughters are, and sees life clear and straight. He discovers his need to be forgiven and learns in humility to be patient.

You and I are like Lear sometimes—used to running things and people, being at the controls, giving orders, managing events, ordering children around, until one day it doesn't work any more. Suddenly a door is slammed, or the bottom falls out, and we are powerless to control our future. Our strength is threatened or destroyed. Our future is in jeopardy. It is then that we begin to cry out with Lear, "You heavens, give me that patience, patience I need!" While we have our power, we don't need to be patient. We can get along without self-knowledge; we can look with contempt upon the weak. When our power is taken from us, in humiliation we may begin to learn humility, to let things and people ripen at their own pace and not to manipulate or hurry them into change. When our power is taken from us, we may learn to respect the unfolding nature of events, to let it be, to let ourselves be, to let others be, to respect the fragility of another person enough to let him shape his own life and find his own fashion of rebirth. We may learn not to insist on our own way—like "I want it now, today, yesterday, my way"—but to yield, to let the life process happen. We may learn to begin to trust the process, not to have to manage or control it, even to believe that it may work out better if many wills work together and somehow God's purpose unfolds through the hidden coordination of it all.

And finally we may learn to pray: "O Lord, renew my strength now, but if not now, then tomorrow, and if not tomorrow, then help me wait in hope and somehow endure whatever happens with patience. Let me reach out to my brothers and sisters who are struggling in their own devastation or powerlessness that they cannot change. Let us be patient with each other, and help me to be patient with myself."

Second, the Lord renews our strength to trust him in the dark. In *The Brothers Karamazov,* Dmitri is the prodigal son/brother. He is the sensual one—generous, wild, outrageous, compassionate, tender. He has the capacity for ecstasy and anguish, guilt and delight, all at once. He says to his brother Alyosha:

> "For I'm a Karamazov. For when I do leap into the pit, I go headlong with my heels up, and am pleased to be falling in that degrading attitude, and pride myself upon it. And in the very depths of that degradation I begin a hymn of praise. Let me be accursed. Let me be vile and base, only let me kiss the hem of the veil in which my God is shrouded. Though I may be following the devil, I am Thy son, O Lord, and I love Thee, and I feel the joy without which the world cannot stand." [6]

I love that man and that prayer and that God. It means to me that no matter what wrong or shame or mess or narrowness of spirit or disgrace or whatever I'm in, however willful, that right from that sin I can cry to God for what I need. I can go to him as I am and know that he still loves me. We can cry to God from right where we are, whatever the nature of our situation. We can go right to him and say, "Here I am with all these ambiguities, with all this weight. Help me."

I used to think that before I could go to God or pray to him I had to get all cleaned up and become acceptable. But I've learned in my own flesh-and-blood life of conflict, betrayal, hurt, and joy, where my pulses throb and my heart aches, that God is right there with me, and with you. We can ask for help and mercy and plead with him for what we need and pray honestly to him. There is no right prayer that we have to pray. There are times when I cannot honestly pray, "Thy will be done," because I'm afraid of the changes he might require and I am unwilling to make those changes. When I feel like that, I don't pray that prayer; I pray out of what I really feel. I lay myself out and God knows who I am. I know he never forsakes me or lets me go, even when I've forsaken him or feel forsaken by him.

Luther's injunction to "trust God and sin on bravely" means that we are free in the love of God to live our humanity fully, boldly—which means inevitably, sinfully—in the knowledge that God goes with us wherever we go, even into the darkest and the most uncertain, unlikely places, with a love for us that is beyond the love of parent for child, or of man for woman. It is a love literally without condition, a love that enables us to pray: "O Lord, though we walk in the valleys filled with shadows, some of our own making, we trust in you without a fear, and we feel the joy without which the world cannot stand."

Finally, the Lord renews our strength to have courage. Courage is grace under pressure. Courage is a tree in a storm, bending low but standing there, rooted in something stronger than the storm. A man wrote me recently:

One evening I was alone in a hotel room, and all at once I felt totally alone, unable to handle things any longer. I wondered what I would do just to make it through the night. But I did make it through, though this was a terrifying experience for me, since I have always projected the image of being a solid rock, able to field anything that life threw my way. I guess being alone in a strange city, cut off from the intimacy of family and home, was just the triggering point. I still wonder how I will react the next time I'm away. The realization that I am vulnerable, that I am capable of suffering emotionally like most everyone else from the pressures exerted on me was a shocking experience. But then perhaps I'm finally gaining some insight into what living is all about, both the heights and depths. My short discussion with you was one of the first times I ever admitted to anyone that things of a deeply personal nature were really getting to me. I'm not in the habit of talking about myself so much. In your position you must certainly feel alone at times. So please remember that a lot of people like me are constantly keeping our arms around you in spirit.

It's OK to discover that you're afraid in a hotel room or at the office, in the family room or at school, in a bedroom, in a jail, or a hospital room. It's OK to admit to each other that things are really getting to us. And when we do—that is, when the courage rolls in—we discover that, together, there is no weakness, no sin, no shame, no sorrow, no tragedy, nothing in all creation that we can't cope with, somehow face, handle, endure, and finally, by God's grace, overcome. We discover, as Camus puts it, "there are more things to admire in men than to despise." [7]

I got a special letter last week which reminded me that God, the God for whom we are waiting, comes to us in strange and unexpected ways and sometimes in the small things and the little people:

Dear Reverend Raines:

I am 12 years old, and I have been going to the church services at 9:15. I can understand you and it makes me feel good to be able to understand someone who can get through to parents and children. You make me feel lucky to be alive and a person. My parents didn't make me write this. I just have been thinking about how great life has been. Many people complain about not being able to get a mink coat or five baseball mitts or something. You have made me feel the good things in life. Thanks.

And thanks to you, my twelve-year-old friend, and thanks to you, my reader friend—and thanks to God who really does renew our strength to be patient, to trust, and to have courage.

O Lord, we need your strength. We feel the pain of our life and of the world. But we feel that joy without which the world cannot stand, too. Sometimes we feel like stretching out our wings and soaring away like eagles flying, and nothing can stop us. Sometimes we feel strength in our legs and we want to run and keep on running and we know that we won't get tired. And sometimes we know we have got to walk. We see more when we walk. And sometimes, Lord, we've got to crawl. Sometimes we've got to just sit there and wait. But we believe in you. Renew our strength—and thanks, thanks to you! Amen.

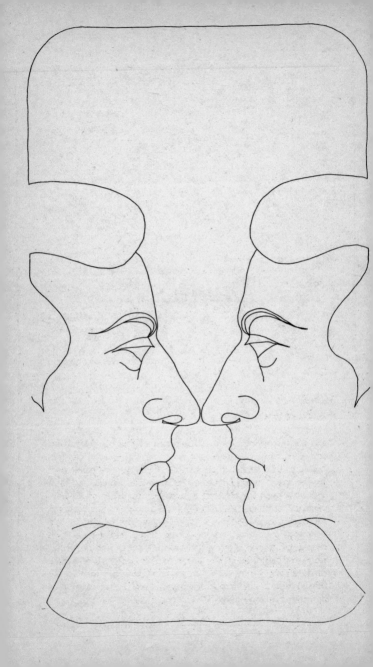

Making It

Making It is the title of a book by Norman Podhoretz. In the preface he writes:

> Let me introduce myself. I am a man who at the precocious age of thirty-five experienced an astonishing revelation: it is better to be a success than a failure. Having been penetrated by this great truth concerning the nature of things, my mind was now open for the first time to a series of corollary perceptions, each one as dizzying in its impact as the Original Revelation itself. Money, I now saw (no one, of course, had ever seen it before) was important: it was better to be rich than poor. Power, I now saw (moving on to higher subtleties) was desirable: it was better to give orders than to take them. Fame, I now saw (how courageous of me not to flinch) was unqualifiedly delicious: it was better to be recognized than anonymous.[1]

Podhoretz says that it took him until he was thirty-five years of age to make these amazing discoveries because he was caught, as many of us may be, in the contradiction between the American gospel of success on the one hand and the Christian gospel of service on the other. Podhoretz resolves the contradiction by coming out four-square for success— unashamed, unapologetic, unguilty success. The book is a witty if not always wise hymn to naked ambition. It suggests a new beatitude to the American scene: "Blessed are the aggressive for they shall reach the top."

Podhoretz would have been pleased with the Zebedee boys, James and John. They were not backward in pushing their ambitions, either. They came to Jesus and said, "Master, we should like you to do us a favour." And Jesus asked, "What is it you want me to do?" And they said, "Grant us the right to sit in state with you, one at your right and the other at your left." [2] No guile, no deal, just a straightforward power play for the top jobs in Jesus' new administration.

Podhoretz recalls a conversation with his teacher, Lionel Trilling, when Trilling asked him what he really wanted to do with himself, what kind of power he was after. Podhoretz replied, "Power? Who ever said anything about power? What did I have to do with power, or it with me?" To which Trilling replied, "Don't be silly, everyone wants power. The only question is what kind." [3]

What kind of power do we want? Over whom? For what purpose? How are we going after it? Or if we already have it, how are we exercising it at home, on the job, in the city?

Norman Mailer once wrote that "everyone was out for all the power he could get at every minute of the day, and that from the most casual confrontation between two people, one emerged with a victory and the other with a defeat." [4] That's red meat.

Making It

I found myself in a conversation at a party the other night with a man I didn't know. I disliked him immediately, and the more I got to know him, the more intensely I disliked him. Almost upon contact, I found myself with combative feelings: "I'm in a struggle here. One of us is going to lose and the other is going to win." Do you find yourself in conversations at home, on the job, at a party, where you do that kind of jockeying for position? I do, sometimes.

What kind of power do we want? Power to get money? Power to get power? To get recognition? To give these things to our kids? Who would we like to dominate or at least neutralize? From whose domination would we like to be freed? It is important to understand the kind of power we want so that we can discover the kinds of engines driving our energies.

James and John knew the power they wanted. It was power in Jesus' administration, which they thought would take political, even military, form. James and John were called the Sons of Thunder because they were members of the Zealots, that band of Jewish patriots and revolutionaries who were committed to the violent overthrow of the hated Roman occupied government. They were somewhat like the patriotic revolutionaries of our own heritage, Thomas Jefferson, Patrick Henry, and others. It is possible that Peter was associated with them for awhile. It is fascinating that Jesus chose these three men—tough, courageous, willing to use violence, if necessary, to bring an end to injustice as they saw it—to be his closest comrades.

What kind of power do we want? Power for our own fulfillment? Success in a cause that matters to us? What does it mean to you and to me to make it?

I was in my teens when I began to realize what "making it" meant to me, and what I had to do to "make it." I went to a rich man's preparatory school in Minneapolis, Minnesota, the city where I grew up. I was a preacher's kid on scholarship. Everybody else was rich, belonged to the city and country clubs, and dominated the social world in Minneapolis. My family was not poor by any means, but we did not belong to that social set. I found that I could not break into it at that school. I got left out, and that made me hurt and angry. Finally it dawned on me the only way to make these boys respect me was to beat them, or as many as I could, at grades, at athletics, at any competition, and demonstrate that I was as good as they were—or maybe a little better! Philosophically, I was buying a meritocracy where status and position are determined by achievement and rejecting a plutocracy where position is determined by wealth and an aristocracy where position is determined by family position. Not only did my family not come over on the Mayflower, but one of our more illustrious forebears on my mother's side was a notorious horse thief in the eastern part of Canada. (But he was a successful horse thief!)

So I learned to compete and win often enough to force my way into their respect, if not affection. I remember one occasion when I was a sophomore and we had what was called there the Fifth Form Declamation Contest. I won it. I can remember standing off by myself in the corner of the library later that day and saying to myself, "I won! I won! I won!" The very fact that I remember the episode so clearly reveals the kind of pressure that I must have felt to succeed in that place. Why did I feel such pressure? Have you ever felt under pressure of that kind?

Upon reflection, there were many factors, but basically it was a longing for self-esteem. My whole environment when I was young was oriented toward succeeding. My parents, from a little town, came to the big city. They felt that pressure, too, and communicated it to us unwittingly. Unconditional love from them was there, but when we achieved, the love really poured in. Indeed, the whole climate of American society put that kind of burden on many of us. We learned in our bones that to feel lovable and loved depended on what we could do rather than on being what we are. I wonder whether our kids are getting this kind of pressure from us, and how much this pressure to succeed operates in our schools, our social climate, our churches.

Further, if you feel loved and valued for what *you* can do, then probably you value and love others for what *they* can do. If you have not come to feel valued just for who you are by the time you get to retirement, it must be a very painful thing when you can't do much any more to feel valued. And what amazing grace it is when there is a moment at home or on the job or with a friend when you suddenly realize that person really does love you just for being you. The burdens are lifted. What a joy that is, and how rarely it happens!

Don't mistake me. I make no apology for excellence, competition, knowledge, skill. I think we all respect someone who does well what he is responsible to do, who has disciplined himself and trained himself to be able to do and be his best. When we need help, when we want a lawyer, teacher, engineer, stockbroker, poet, plumber, or whatever else, we want the best. It is sad when any person, young or old, sits on his power and wastes his tremendous potentiality, when he fails to mine his own gold and just lets it waste away until he forgets where the mine shafts are.

But the drive to succeed, to make it, becomes destructive when winning takes precedence over everything else. Vince Lombardi, the late great football coach, said, "Winning isn't everything; winning is the only thing." He was a great football coach, and winning above all may win a lot of football games or sell a lot of soap, but it may not make for a winning combination in the family, on the job, in the church or in the nation. For somehow the win/lose thing has got to be replaced by a win/win thing. When there are one or two losers in a family, the whole family loses. When people on the job or in the city or in a group divide into winning groups and losing groups, then the whole community is a losing community. Somehow there has to be room in a family and on the job and in the city and in the society for every person and group to have a piece of the action which he regards as significant and fulfilling. This happens when competition makes room for cooperation.

In my own limited experience I have learned—and perhaps you have, too—that the compulsion to win, to succeed, to beat the other guy, company, be Number One, whatever the cost, can make you insensitive, hard, unfeeling, unaware of how other people feel, out of touch with your own feelings. You begin to use people, to exploit them to fulfill your goals and you learn how to dominate either overtly or covertly, to control or manage by one means or another. The worst thing of all is that you may not even be aware of doing it!

When you do that, people get angry. They strike back with whatever power is at their disposal; as the other disciples got angry with James and John for their power grab; as a great friend of mine got angry with me one time. He was a layman in our church in Philadelphia, the head of the pastoral relations committee, and a wonderful guy. We were working together on a project in the church. I have referred to this earlier, or at least to the letter he wrote. He told me that it seemed to him that I was not comfortable unless the reins were in my hands and I was in control. Therefore, I tended to use lay leadership as a façade to get my own purposes accomplished rather than as a dynamic, cooperative force to get a mutual purpose achieved. I was shocked because I had not been aware that he thought I was trying to control him, much less that he was angry about it. And I was scared because I wasn't aware that I was trying to control him. Maybe there was some distance between my image of myself and the real me. The last line of his letter read, "I hope it is obvious that if I didn't love you and the church, I wouldn't have taken the time to hunt and peck my way through this. It would have been much easier to say the hell with you."

We had lunch and we talked and I listened and I learned something about myself from my friend who cared enough about me to tell me. I think I have since grown a little bit in my understanding of my own motives and in the willingness, sometimes in the gladness, to help other people fulfill their dreams as well as working out my own. But every now and then something happens which reminds me that the old pattern is operating again. It makes me feel that maybe there is some kind of basic character structure that gets formed in us very early and which, while we may become aware of it, moderate it, change it a little bit, still remains there. We have to learn how to live with it and transform its energies into creative actions.

My friend gave me a hint of the sort of thing that Jesus was talking about to James and John and the other disciples when they were trying to get ahead. Jesus told them, "You know that in the world the recognized rulers lord it over their subjects, and their great men make them feel the weight of authority. That is not the way with you; among you, whoever wants to be great must be your servant, and whoever wants to be first must be the willing slave of all." [5]

That is a switch. Most of us would rather fight than switch. Remember the gospel according to Leo Durocher: "Nice guys finish last." Who wants to be last, least, lowest? Nobody! So we have a problem. We have a paradox. How do we relate the drive to succeed to the call to serve?

A friend of mine had an experience in an encounter group some time ago, a group that lasted several days. He gained fresh insights into himself and that paradox. He writes:

> Pecking orders repel me. In the past I've dealt with this by being aloof, refusing to peck or be pecked ... yet somehow a body ought to be able to rap with another body in the context of traditional systems and enjoy it. Maybe instead of a pecking order there could be an order of servanthood ... that flows both up and down the corporate ladder. "Making it" for me seems to have something to do with helping. My encounter group experience gave me some insight into "making it." I very definitely made it there ... that is, I was accepted ... and I felt accepted ... that I was making it ... how did this happen? I asked for help and I got it. *And I helped others.* That was okay. I discovered serving as a means to power, the power of self-acceptance. There were no Hitler types around coercing others into belonging. But we were all leaders, all making it, because we helped each other. If there was one leader who stood out, it was the facilitator of our group, but that was because he was the most skillful at helping others.

Great insights there for the family, the job, the nation. Making it in the deepest human sense is something that we can only do together. I cannot make it by myself, not really. We need each other in order to make it. Power differentials exist and will continue to exist. Yet in whatever structure we find ourselves, each of us can be a facilitator rather than a dominator, be it president or secretary or whatever. Each of us needs to acknowledge that he needs the specialness of the

other person, both those above us and below us on the hier-
archical scale. We can overcome the realities of power structures humanly by acknowledging that we all need each other
and that nobody is self-sufficient. I am only part of what I
could be without you—white and black, right and left, young
and old, parents and kids, employer and employees, America
and other nations. We all need each other in some kind of
interdependence in which being Number One is no longer
important. Rather the important thing is to find a cooperative
style where each of us affirms the others and is affirmed in
turn for his own value, his own unique gift, and where the
style is not domination but facilitation, competition in cooperation.

This is to acknowledge that you and I each sit on a load
of power, much of which we are not using, not releasing,
not living. Each of us has charisma. Each of us has spirit.
Just as each of us has a unique fingerprint, so each of us has
a unique inner personal gift. We are all the poorer if we do
not encourage it to be released in others nor release our own.
Jesus is calling us into a new community where leadership will
be measured in terms of effective facilitation of others; where
each of us will find the fulfillment of his own dreams as he
encourages others to the fulfillment of theirs; where our task
will be not to share our riches with others but to reveal their
riches to them—and where my power of self-esteem, my
fullness of human being, will come to me as yours comes to
you.

Making love is a central human symbol of succeeding by
mutually serving one another, of finding one's own fulfillment in the fulfillment of another, of mutual facilitation. In a
spiritual sense, then, making it in human terms is making love
happen at home, on the job, in the city—and finding the paradox of success through serving.

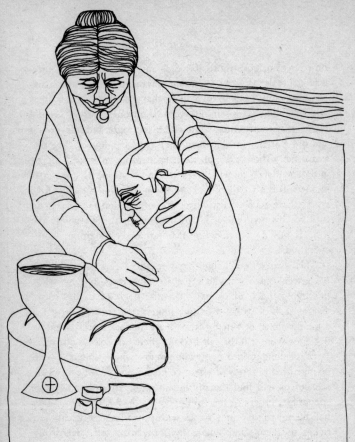

*It's OK
to Need Comfort*

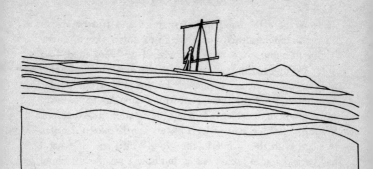

EACH HUMAN being is alone. We experience our aloneness in rending events or moments—the loss of health, of a job, of a mate, of a friend, the death of a hope. Some layer of comfort in our lives is ripped away, and there we are, having to go it alone. Our aloneness rises up like an iceberg in front of us— an empty chair, an empty bed, an empty office, an empty or aching heart.

Sometimes we experience our aloneness as an annoying, free-floating itch with no place to scratch, a yearning deep within us that will not let us rest, a restlessness to know and to be known wholly, to touch our own deeps and the deeps of another, a restlessness to reach out and feel the heartbeat of creation.

Sometimes our aloneness gets heavy and is like a burden

made up of a thousand little irritations and frustrations or minor disappointments which weigh us down, down, down.

One morning, some time ago, when I was very tired, I sat in on a group meeting at the church. Several weeks of going to breakfasts, luncheons, dinners with groups of our people, listening intently to their concerns, trying to be sensitive and responsive to criticism had left me emotionally exhausted. With my psychic energy level lower than I realized, I began to share with the people in the group a little bit of what I had been doing in recent weeks and how I was feeling about what was happening in the life of the congregation. I soon sensed sympathy, understanding, coming at me from the faces and gestures of some of the people in that room. And as you do when you feel you are in a climate of comfort, I unconsciously let my inner guard down and shared my feelings more personally than I had intended. My burden began to rise in me; I was filling up. Bowing my head in order to pray, I found that I couldn't say anything for fear of losing control of myself. Somewhere in me a little dam had broken. I struggled in the silence for a composure that did not return. Finally, I croaked out an "Amen" and left.

Comfort had touched me and opened me and made me vulnerable. Criticism or hostility I could have handled with the back of my hand, but comfort undid me and I was too tired to resist it. God comforted me through the comfort of some of my friends.

Whoever else God is and whatever else he does, in a primary, continuing deep, primordial sense, he is the comforting presence and power in your life and in mine. And the incredible Good News is that he takes the initiative in coming to you and to me. We don't have to do anything. We don't have to make anything right. He is coming to you and me as we are, where we are, in our aloneness, in our need for comfort.

You know, it's OK to need to be comforted. Though I know that, it's still a little hard for me not to feel ashamed when I need to be comforted. Someone should teach us that it is as blessed to receive comfort as it is to give comfort, that it is as human to need to be consoled as to console. Having identified with my strength for most of my life, only lately have I been discovering something of my weakness. Many of us are raised by profession, by parenthood, by persuasion, to be comforters of others. The Christian syndrome puts tremendous emphasis on that. We often then are holding another and seldom being held. But it's OK sometimes to need to be held. Indeed, we become richer, deeper, warmer, more understanding, more compassionate and patient and humble human beings when we understand and acknowledge our own need of receiving love as well as giving it.

What if we need comfort somewhere in our life today? *God comforts us through the comfort of a spouse or a friend or a colleague or some special person.*

Years ago I was in conversation with a woman who told me about her fear of herself and her relationships with other people. She began to tell me about a friend she was getting to know and how much he meant to her. Then several days later a letter came in which she said: "When I am with him, I feel cared for and protected as I never have before. When I'm with him, the fear that I was voicing to you when we talked recently is absent. It always gives way to delight. His care makes me gentle and confident." It is so beautiful, isn't it?—the image of the comfort that we can give each other. And the image of the comfort that we can find in God if we can entrust ourselves to him in that way.

We all need comfort—even Jesus did. And to me one of the

most poignant things he ever said is this: "Foxes have holes, and birds of the air have nests; but the Son of Man has nowhere to lay his head." [1] No home, no wife, no children. One of the tender touches in *Jesus Christ, Superstar* is the comfort that Mary Magdalene gives to Jesus. While the interpretation is uncertain historically, it does express his need as a human being, as a man, to be understood, to be comforted.

I feel closer to Jesus, knowing that because he had a lonesome valley to walk through, too, he understands yours and mine. I feel closer to God because of him, because Jesus is the humanity of God made tangible and available and vulnerable for us. Bread and wine are physical, tangible symbols of his comfort that literally go into us. He is in us, with us, for us—this word of comfort made flesh in us, in our lives and our hearts and our life together.

Whenever you are with someone and you feel cared for, protected; when your fear changes to delight and you are left gentle, confident—then know that whoever has been with you, God has also been with you. For he is the source of all comfort that comes to us. He comforts us through a spouse or a friend or some special person.

God comforts us also in the depths of our own inner being, our private aloneness, deep down.

My mother and father were with us last Thanksgiving after having been in Independence, Iowa, for a few days. They grew up in that little town of 4500 people, and Dad said he went back there to worship in the church in which he was raised and buy a tombstone and raise a little hell (hard to imagine doing the latter in Independence!). They are great people—they don't criticize us; they don't criticize our kids. They don't even criticize the way we raise our kids. What more can you ask of grandparents than that!

I was reminded, however, of a time last summer when my

mother confided to me, "Bob, I feel that I wasn't as important to you as your father when you were growing up, that you related primarily to him. And I wondered sometimes if I really mattered very much to you at all." I was astounded; I had no inkling that my mother had ever had any feelings of that kind.

As I reflected on our family life, I realized that my father was a very dominant personality in our home and in our environment. We all felt the sheer power of his being. His sun shone so brightly and warmly and brilliantly that some of those who lived close to him often felt they were in his shadow. In recent years as his sun is shining with less power, perhaps more gently, my mother's sun has been rising. She's been hit with Women's Lib in her late sixties and early seventies. She has often said that she felt like she was "Dad's wife" during all those earlier years. Always having been introduced as "his wife," now she is insisting on exploring her own independent being. It's a beautiful thing to watch though it's painful, too, sometimes.

I could and did acknowledge to her my gratitude for the unconditional "no-matter-what-you-do-you're-my-boy" kind of loyalty that she gave me over those years. It built into my bones whatever self-confidence is there. But I saw in a fresh light how, as you get older, you need to be reassured that you still matter to the people who matter to you. You watch the world, the church, your family going their own way. You know it's good and right and that they have to do it, but you find yourself wondering whether you matter much any more. You need to know that you're special to the people who are special to you. You need to be assured that you are somebody. You need to be comforted. And further, I saw in a fresh way how important it is all through the years for each of us to discern and follow his own light, to explore his own trails, to test his own deeps, to put his feet out as far as he can in the world and walk by himself so that he knows that he can walk alone, that he is somebody all by himself.

I'm coming to savor my own solitude more, to want to be alone more in nature, in reflection and reading. I've been reading lately a book by Rainer Maria Rilke called *Letters to a Young Poet*. There are nuggets on every page. He says:

> *Everything* is gestation and then bringing forth. To let each impression and each germ of a feeling come to completion wholly in itself, in the dark, in the inexpressible, the unconscious, beyond the reach of one's intelligence, and await with deep humility and patience the birth-hour of a new clarity: that alone is living.[2]

That's living from the inside out! That's the confidence that God really is in you and in me, to comfort, to sustain your very fragile but very strong spirit.

Come with me now for a moment on a fantasy trip. Close your eyes. Imagine that you are on an island. It's beautiful; the weather is lovely. You have everything you need to eat and drink, and you have clothes. But there is no other living being on the island. You are alone. As you walk along the beach, you think you sight a speck on the horizon,—yes, it's a raft and it is coming closer. And someone is on it. Yes, you can recognize who it is!

Who is it? Who is it who is coming to comfort you in your aloneness? Maybe you saw one face, maybe many. Whomever you saw may be significant in your life. God may be coming to comfort you through that person or persons.

O Lord, though I walk alone through my island valley of shadows, I will fear no evil, for you are with me. And you comfort me in my aloneness.

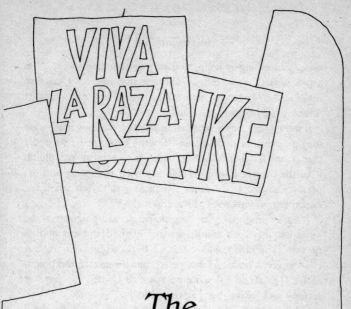

The
Confidence to Change

In Lorraine Hansberry's play *The Sign in Sidney Brustein's Window*, Iris, a mixed-up but sensitive girl, is married to Sidney, a restless dreamer who has failed in many ventures and now operates a little weekly newspaper fighting a corrupt political machine. They live in an apartment in Greenwich Village in New York City. One night the pressures and problems build up and get to them. Picking up his guitar, Sidney begins to pick out his dreams on it while Iris wanders aimlessly. Early in the morning, in the soft light and muted sounds of the still sleeping city, they end up sitting together on the fire escape talking of those things in the human heart which seem to come out of hiding in such moments. Almost in tears, Iris whispers out all the fears and disappointments of her life. As she gropes to put into words her unformed longings, she says, "Something is happening to me, changing me. . . . You know what I want, Sidney? I'm twenty-nine. . . . I want to *make* it, Sid. *Whatever* that means and *however* it means it! That's what I want." [1]

Twenty-nine, nineteen, thirty-nine, seventy-nine—that longing aches in each of us: "I want to make it, whatever that means for me; I want to taste life to the full and plumb it to the depths. I want to find my own real being and experience myself at the roots. I want to give myself wholly to something, to somebody. I want to make it."

It's a longing that gets more desperate and poignant as the years lengthen into middle age and beyond and our options narrow. The time comes when we begin to feel our last few chances are at hand. As one person put it recently and poignantly, "I'm afraid I'll wake up some day when I'm sixty or seventy and realize that I've missed it!"

What is "it"? The "it" we want to make and are afraid to miss? Is it financial security, professional or vocational success, seeing our kids turn their promise into reality, finding our own authentic selfhood and living it fully and honestly, knowing deep sexual fulfillment, finding creative work that releases the unique gifts inside us, losing ourselves in some purpose or cause which is bigger than we are and that is worth everything we've got—even our life? Yes, all that and yet more, much more.

But whatever it means to you and me to make it, not to miss it in our desperate dreams, there comes the time or times when we feel no matter what our external achievements or success may be or appear to be, that we're not making it. We're missing it, like a child with his nose pressed to the window pane and watching life go by outside there. Bye bye, baby, bye bye.

Paul watched life pass him by in that prison in Rome where he waited in uncertainty for two years, finally to hear a sentence of death. As his options narrowed down and finally closed off, he wrote the congregation he loved more than any other, the people in Philippi, pouring out his trouble and his hopes to them, sharing his gratitude for them. He said: "I have learned, in whatever state I am, to be content. I know how to be abased, and I know how to abound; in any and all circumstances I have learned the secret of facing plenty and hunger, abundance and want. I can do all things in him who strengthens me." [2]

Strength for anything through the One who gives us inward power. How can we get in touch with that One who gives us inward power, so that no matter what our external circumstances, we too may experience that deep unshakable confidence flowing in like an underground stream of the self, like an inner tidal wave affirming us and singing, "Yes, I'm with you and for you—I love you; you are precious to me— you are beautiful"?

Sometimes the One who gives us inward power takes us by surprise in some strange unlikely place and rolls his tidal waves over our fear and tear-stained fences. A year ago at the National Training Lab in Bethel, Maine, in the context of an encounter group that lasted for several days, some friends pulled this plank and that plank out of my defenses, until all at once my defenses were swept away in a torrent of soundless sobbing which left me heaving with that inward power. I hadn't cried for years—except perhaps a few tears in a movie, or a really good commercial! I think perhaps I had not cried, since I was a child, for myself, for my own pains and hurts. Somehow I had willed and walled them away and refused to acknowledge and suffer them. So I cried there with those friends. I cried for that aching longing deep in me, the fear that somehow I wasn't making it, that I was missing it. And in the crying came relief and the release of that inward power which rolled through me and assured me that I was precious and beloved just as I was—that I didn't have to make it; somebody had already made it for me. I didn't have to prove something to somebody, because somebody had already approved of me. An experience of amazing grace! Have you had such a time lately?

Sometimes the One who gives us inward power takes us by surprise in the last place we might expect it—in church on Sunday morning! Someone wrote me recently:

> I remember a poignant Sunday not too long ago. My depression engulfed me, a deep, dark fog with no glimmer of light. It took every ounce of energy I had just to get up and go to church, but I needed help. I got it! The Sunday before you had gathered the congregation's prayers and now you mentioned you loved a man because he was still searching. I knew you loved me because I was still searching, too—blindly, to be sure. I needed that. To have someone say that at that time was priceless. I felt so unworthy of anybody's care because I was in such a hole with no ladder. Somebody cared when I couldn't be reached. Now, I know that many care. My family most of all, and I feel that a lot of people from the church really give a damn about me, too. Without that knowledge, I'd still be in that hole instead of halfway out. I needed that to give me a handhold and a toehold..."

We come together on Sunday for the purpose of giving each other a handhold, a toehold. It's hard for me to believe that God really likes me, takes me as I am, but when I see your face and when I join my hand to yours (and maybe it works both ways), somehow that inward power gets released and can flow. And there's a deep kind of mutual support that comes to us, sometimes anyway.

The congregation I presently serve has freed me to make some little changes in my own behavior. It may seem a small thing, but I wanted to take my clerical robe off, and did so. I felt that the robe covered me up in some way, separating me from the people and wrapping me like a straitjacket into my role as a clergyman. It wasn't anybody's problem but mine, but it *was* mine. So for me not to wear that robe on Sunday morning means that I feel more open, vulnerable, and available in my own humanity to the congregation. It is my little hangup, a tiny little gesture, as though I were saying to God, "OK, Lord, now I'm going to be a little more naked before you. Hit me with that inward power. Shake me and remake me some way or other."

I don't know what your little hangup may be, what little black mask or robe or habit or façade you might be ready to get rid of. Maybe there is some little gesture you might make just for yourself, some little decision right now, by which you could say to God, "OK, I want to set that little phony thing aside now. Hit me with that inward power. I'm ready. Roll into me, do with me whatever you're going to do."

A friend of mine was staying overnight in the home of a Yugoslav pastor and his wife and three boys some time ago. Two of the boys were handsome, strong young men. They were going to the university and showing high promise. The third boy, twenty years old, was over in the corner of the room, playing with his toys. My friend asked if he might take a picture of the family, thinking of the parents and the two normal boys. But the father said to him, "Wait a moment until I get him ready." Then the picture was taken with the retarded boy in the center. My friend said to me, "I never show that picture to anyone. We can't exploit human tragedy. But I learned something from that father about what it means to belong to the family. No child was missing from that picture, not one."

You and I belong to the Father's family. And no one of us is missing from that picture, not one. Each of us feels at times the idiot in himself, feels himself to be ugly, unacceptable, loathsome, outcast. But you and I are in the center of that picture, just as we are, beloved by the Father. Let us feel now that inward power moving in us, like an inner tidal wave singing affirmation, "Yes, I'm with you and for you. I love you. You beautiful idiot, you. You are free now to change and make changes."

It takes confidence to change, to move from one time or style of life to another, to let some parts of our role, our being, fade and others grow and develop. Someone wrote me recently, "My husband returned Saturday from taking our daughter to start her college career. Then Tuesday evening we moved our other daughter into an apartment near campus. So many people seem surprised that I'm not beside myself with the children gone. I love my children deeply, and for twenty years I've been responsible for their needs. Now it's time for the 'mom' part of their cocoon to go and for them to fly. They know I'll be here if and when they need me. But my husband and I are alone, beautifully alone. How great to have all that time for him, for us. It's kind of like when we started out twenty-three years ago, only better."

It takes confidence to change when you're afraid to take risks, afraid to say yes and walk into the unknown future because you can't control that future. It takes confidence to change when you're crippled by an inability to know your own mind, when you've made one mistake and you're scared silly you'll make another. So you stay on dead center and don't do anything. But when we join hands together and begin to walk together, that inward power begins to flow again through us, and we feel and know that we have the strength to decide, to say yes or no, to try to fly!

It takes confidence to change a congregation or a city or a state or a company or a country. Kenneth Clark in his lucid book *Civilisation* writes:

> Civilisation requires a modicum of material prosperity— enough to provide a little leisure. But, far more, it requires confidence—confidence in the society in which one lives, belief in its philosophy, belief in its laws and confidence in one's own mental powers. The way in which the stones of the Pont du Gard are laid is not only a triumph of technical skill, but shows a vigorous belief in law and discipline. Vigour, energy, vitality: all the great civilisations—or civilising epochs—have had a weight of energy behind them.[3]

Because you and I have deep confidence in the dreams of our founding fathers for this country and because we believe in our nation's capacity to make those dreams of liberty and justice for all come true, we can acknowledge the mistakes and failures we make when we make them. We may become impatient at the snail-slow pace of making our country's dreams come true, but we have no right, as Christians, to be in despair. While our power is limited and finite and inadequate, there is an inward power surging in history, as there is in our own personal histories, which sometimes rushes through the ugliness and pain and brutality to carry us on and through. It is the power of God who gives us strength to work today for the day when our alabaster cities will be undimmed by those unnecessary human tears, and America will be as beautiful in truth as she is in our dreams!

In this confidence we are free to make creative changes and to become change facilitators. To be a Christian is to be a change facilitator for God. Sometimes we seek to facilitate change in a system or an institution or structure of which we are a part from the inside, when we have a position of power, of leverage, of influence.

Maybe you are in a position of influence, let's say, in a corporation or a union or a bank or a law firm or a real estate firm or a company or whatever it may be. There are laws forbidding racial discrimination to which your firm, of course, is subject. There are always ways to make token responses to a law—that one or others—to get around it if you want to. Or people like you and me can decide, can choose to be leaders not only in abiding by the letter of the law but in living by the spirit of the law and by making changes in our employment or membership or lending or whatever practices, going the second mile and then the third mile, and having great delight in helping to shape the future. The future where we are going is open and inclusive. The past where we've been is closed and exclusive. Who wants to cling to a dying past? Wouldn't we rather be flyers and fly into the future—God's future? What wrong is within our power to begin to make right today, this week, this month?

Sometimes we have to seek to facilitate change in a given system or institution or structure from the outside because that's where we are. We're not on the inside. We do not have a position of power. We have a position of powerlessness with regard to this system or structure.

Ralph Nader is a good example of a man who facilitates change from a position of no institutional power save the power of public opinion. You and I may or may not like Nader, and probably few of us would espouse all his views—or, for that matter, all your views or all my views. But undoubtedly he is a modern David, taking on the Goliaths of big government, big business, big labor, and effecting changes through the power of public opinion and the pressure of law. One of the great things about Nader, in my opinion, is his deep respect for law and his confidence that the system has transforming, reforming capacities within it. He has a puritan insistence that even big government, big business, and big labor should obey the law and be responsible to the society which enriches them.

So a number of young and intelligent and very able lawyers work for him at six, seven, or eight thousand dollars a year, which is the kind of commitment I have to respect a lot—a real commitment to the public welfare at some considerable personal financial sacrifice. We can understand why it is that the people outside the positions of power and influence in the systems and structures of the day—the blacks, the poor, the young, and so on—have to seek change by means of public protest. That's the only route that is open to them. And it is abundantly clear that the monumental changes in attitude, in consciousness, in recent years in this country toward the Vietnam war, pollution, racial injustice, university and school reform are in large part due to those human-rights, human-liberation movements of the recent decade, not only in America but in other countries across the world. We can believe that we shall overcome the evils in ourselves and in our society and in our structures through the power of God who gives us the confidence to change. What rights or reforms can we, from a position outside, from a position of powerlessness, commend to the citadels of power today—this day?

Do we want to make it? Do we have the confidence to change ourselves and the world around us a little? Can we hear the words that keep coming, "I am with you and for you, you beautiful idiot, you. I love you!"

Embraceable You

SOME YEARS ago a seventeen-year-old boy with a record as a juvenile delinquent wrote his parents a letter at Christmas time.

Dear Folks:

Thank you for everything, but I am going to Chicago and try and start some kind of new life. You asked me why I did those things and why I gave you so much trouble, and the answer is easy for me to give you, but I am wondering if you will understand.

Remember when I was about six or seven and I used to want you to just listen to me? I remember all the nice things you gave me for Christmas and my birthday and I was really happy with the things—for about a week—at the time I got the things, but the rest of the time during the year I really didn't want presents. I just wanted all the time for you to listen to me like I was somebody who felt things too, because I remember even when I was young I felt things. But you said you were busy.

Mom, you are a wonderful cook, and you had everything so clean and you were tired so much from doing all those things that made you busy; but, you know something, Mom? I would have liked crackers and peanut butter just as well if you had only sat down with me a while during the day and said to me: "Tell me all about it so I can maybe help you understand!"

And when Donna came I couldn't understand why everyone made so much fuss because I didn't think it was my fault that her hair is curly and her skin so white, and she doesn't have to wear glasses with such thick lenses. Her grades were better too, weren't they? If Donna ever has children, I hope you will tell her to just pay some attention to the one who doesn't smile very much because that one will really be crying inside. And when she's about to bake six dozen cookies, to make sure first that the kids don't want to tell her about a dream or a hope or something, because thoughts are important, too, to small kids, even though they don't have so many words to use when they tell about what they have inside them.

I think that all the kids who are doing so many things that grown-ups are tearing out their hair worrying about are really looking for somebody that will have time to listen a few minutes and who really and truly will treat them as they would a grown-up who might be useful to them, you know—polite to them. If you folks had ever said to me: "Pardon me" when you interrupted me, I'd have dropped dead! If anybody asks you where I am, tell them I've gone looking for somebody with time because I've got a lot of things I want to talk about.

Love to all,
Your Son [1]

Are we thinking, "I'm just too busy to listen to my kids,

my spouse, my friends, parents, trying to tell me what's going on inside them—a hope, a dream or something? I just have too much to do, buy, remember, write, arrange. Cards not sent yet, bills already coming in, parties we're invited to and parties we weren't invited to, relatives coming on like gangbusters. The tree—get it, decorate it. Church on Christmas Eve. I'm just too busy to listen, too late, too tired . . ."?

The other night—or rather, early in the morning while it was still dark—our six-year-old Bobby crawled into bed with us. My first inclination was to send him back to his own bed. I was irritated at being wakened and was afraid I wouldn't get back to sleep. He kept saying he was afraid of something, so reluctantly I pulled him beside me, his small body snuggled next to mine, his head in the curve of my neck, my arm around him, cupping his round boy's bottom with my hand. We lay there for awhile being comfortable together, and he began to tell me what he was afraid of. He was afraid that he wouldn't bring the right kind of paper to school the next day. The teacher had told him to bring a special kind of paper, and he couldn't remember what kind it was. So we went over all the kinds of paper we could think of. Wrapping paper—no, towel paper—no, toilet paper—no. We just couldn't get the right kind of paper. (Later we discovered it was tissue paper!) But anyhow he seemed to feel better just talking about it, and somehow he felt assured we'd find out in time the right kind of paper. He suggested that we play a rhyming game where I say a word like "street" and he rhymes it with "eat," "meat," etc. We played that game for awhile and dozed a bit. Before long, it was time to get up.

Paul put the Good News of Christmas in a sentence when he said, "For I am convinced that there is . . . nothing in all creation that can separate us from the love of God in Christ

Jesus our Lord." [2] Jesus is the human way God chose to get close to us, to pull us beside him to put his arm around us. Jesus comes to us right in our fear, our loneliness, our separation, our feeling of being forgotten. Jesus is listening to our hopes and dreams, everything that is going on inside us.

Christmas only intensifies what is going on inside you and me and what is happening to us. If things are great, then Christmas heightens our joy. If there is anger or hurt in the family or an ache in the heart that nobody else can really share, then Christmas drives that pain deeper in search of some new kind of suffering-joy.

A card came from Ann, only seven months since her husband George died, alone at Christmas with her three little girls. Why George? Why now? So able, such promise. How is she going to make it? How did she put it on the card? "Some say to me, 'This first Christmas without your husband will be hard for you.' Probably it will be, but without Christmas my life would be impossible."

What spirit that woman has! She really believes God's love came through at Christmas, is coming through to her now, that nothing—not even her husband's death—can separate her or him from the love of God. Somehow where fear, pain, ache are the worst, that is where Jesus comes first. And that is fantastic. Christmas makes our life—whatever it is—possible, no matter what happens to us. Nothing can prevent God from putting his arm around us. That is what Jesus means.

It reminded me of Dietrich Bonhoeffer, the German theologian who was in prison at the time of the Second World War in Hitler's Germany and separated from his loved ones until the time of his execution. He wrote letters to them and he learned while he was in prison to live through his ache. He writes words which may help you and me, whatever our ache and whatever our experience of separation. He says:

We must suffer the unutterable agony of separation and feel the longing until it makes us sick. . . . It is nonsense to say that God fills the gap: He does not fill it, but keeps it empty so that our communion with another may be kept alive, even at the cost of pain . . . the dearer and richer our memories, the more difficult the separation. But gratitude converts the pangs of memory into a tranquil joy. . . . We must not wallow in our memories or surrender to them, just as we don't gaze all the time at a valuable present, but get it out from time to time, and for the rest hide it away as a treasure that we know is there all the time. . . . It has been borne in upon me here with peculiar force that a concrete situation can always be mastered, and that only fear and anxiety magnify them to an immeasurable degree beforehand. From the moment we awake until we fall asleep we must commend our loved ones wholly and unreservedly to God and leave them in his hands, transforming our anxiety for them into prayers on their behalf.[3]

I am not there yet, but I want to be. I want to try to offer my ache and anxiety to God hoping that maybe he'll make prayers out of them, take all the might-have-beens and cannot-bes, take me as I am, take you as you are, put his arm around us, listen to our dreams and our hopes until we know that somehow we're going to be all right.

It's like the phone call between a guy and his girl (you've had calls like this) where he is rattling on about his problems so hard and fast and not listening to her until she says insistently, "Did you hear what I said?" And he says, "No," and she says, "I love you!" He says, "Oh!" And it's like the sun cutting through the fog.

Jesus is God's son, shining through our fog and saying to us, "I love you." If only we can stop being busy long enough to listen at the phone, at the desk, kitchen table, the bedroom, to hear a song that someone is trying to sing into our heart, to look for a star in the skies or see the stars in someone's eyes.

A letter came from a woman in our congregation whose first baby was recently born, sharing her reflections as she watched her baby sleeping one night. She wrote:

> It is late and as I listen to the silent noises, my mind is something like a huge funnel with a very small opening. There are millions of things that want to come out and yet they are hampered by my narrowness and the limitations words place on feelings. . . . A free child has been born and I am watching her sleep. I have no expectations for her. How can I? When she is my age, it will be 2001, a space odyssey. So how can there be expectations—only joy of this moment. But I can look back over the past, before Jennifer, and reflect on those people who brought me to this point tonight. I want to say thank you to many people but I can't find vocal cords strong enough to shout it or words meaningful enough to say it. There is the free child's father who, like me, is struggling with how to be free himself. There are friends who have sung songs, painted pictures, laughed and cried with us and for us. Parents and friends who did the mundane tasks as a way to say they cared . . . arms, words, hands, gifts and cards all saying "Welcome" to the free child and "I love you" to us. With Thanksgiving past and Christmas near, I have found new meaning in being thankful and a new unbelievable meaning in the joy there is in the birth of a child. This Christmas the old words will come alive and inside of me there will be an endless thank you![4]

What joy that the ultimate power of the universe is saying to us in a thousand ways, if we can only hear, "I love you, no matter what happens to you, no matter what you do or where you go, I love you and I always will, and nothing can ever separate you from me." That is all the news we need. That is enough, more than enough, to base a life on, to offer a death to. And it is Jesus who persuades us that maybe it just might be so—not just his words to us, but our experience of him together. He is the one who tempts us to hope and to follow him into the future, that hook-nosed, bearded Jew who broke conventions, crossed boundaries, met people where they were and took them where they never thought they could go. That Jesus—he's the one who haunts us into hoping that there is someone somewhere in the galaxies whirling out there and in here listening to our dreams and hopes, that there is mystery in us as well as chemistry, that there is a living word in our dying flesh, and our ending is our beginning, that nothing in all creation can separate us from his love, the love of him who, even now, as on that first Christmas, is reaching out to embrace you and me.

Some years ago a beautiful woman in her sixties shared a remarkable experience which is a kind of parable of God's Christmas embrace in his world. She wrote:

It happened during the Christmas season. I was walking down Chestnut Street when I noticed a large group of people concentrating on some object. As I approached, I saw a little girl about seven years old who was obviously lost, sobbing and bewildered. She was pulling away from all those who tried to take her hand and comfort her, including the young policeman who was endeavoring to interest her in his horse. Something impelled me to walk through that crowd of people and when I reached the inner circle, I stooped down and reached out my arms without saying a word. Almost instantly the little girl turned around and our eyes met. Then she put out her arms, straight out just as I held mine—and came toward me. She was a large child and ordinarily I would not attempt to lift one so heavy, but as she came confidently and unhesitatingly into my arms, I enfolded her and stood up. She entwined her arms and legs around my body and struggled to get closer and closer until we were almost a single figure. We stood in that position for a long time without uttering a single word. I did not ask her name, nor did she say anything at all to me, but she was quiet, relaxed, and contented. The small crowd around us did not move or converse. There was complete silence.

It must have been fully ten minutes that we clung together before something made me turn and I saw a young woman with blue eyes—I remember so poignantly those calm eyes—standing close by. She had evidently just approached us. It was then I uttered the first words I had spoken since discovering the little one. "Does she belong to you?"

"Yes," the woman replied, and then the child disengaged herself from my arms, quietly slid down to the sidewalk, and silently the two walked off together. The mother did not thank me nor did the child give me a glance. They disappeared in the holiday throng as though nothing at all had happened. I turned and began walking away and felt a peculiar exaltation and buoyancy I had never experienced before. My chest almost ached with the wonder that swelled within me, for I knew I had been a vehicle for a divine purpose—and that miracles do happen!"

May such miracles happen to you, embraceable you!

Kiss the
Joy as It Flies

SOMEHOW the last few days have capsuled for me a year in which—as I suppose it always is—joy and sorrow have walked hand in hand. On Tuesday there was a funeral for a sixteen-year-old boy who died a tragic death a week ago. On Wednesday there was a heavy discussion of our church budget for the next year, our priorities, purposes, and hopes for the New Year. On Thursday in late morning I married two people in mid-course in their lives—their second marriage. Later in the afternoon I baptized two fresh little human beings who have appeared on this earth. Friday night was the wedding of two young people who are going to spend the first year of their life together living in a cabin in the woods on the West Coast.

Later that night was the New Year's Eve dance of our

high schoolers, and, still later in the evening, a New Year's Eve
party where there were a few old friends, but many strangers.
As we passed over into the New Year from the old, I felt no
exhilaration at all, but a pensiveness and a pondering.

What time is it in my life?

I want to touch the tapestry of my life, melt its meaning,
taste its fruit. I reach for permanence only to taste transience.

> Bitter is the beauty
> when tender is the time.

What time is it in your life? What the bitter, what the
beauty?

We reach for permanence as time goes by. One time Peggy
and I drove into West Rutland, Vermont, where she was
born. She was eager to see the old homestead, the huge white
frame house with its generous, protective tree in front and
gracious green lawn stretching out back in the pleasant, pros-
perous suburban town. But when we reached West Rutland,
it was only to find that today it is a ghost town, its shabby
buildings for sale, for rent, for demolition. Finally, unbeliev-
ably, on the right street, we experienced the disappointment
of coming up to a rather small, unprepossessing frame dwell-
ing, peeling gray paint, scrubby old tree in the front, a patch
of crab grass in the back. We got out of there fast.

What tricks memory, time, change, play on us. Nostalgia,
which tastes good at the first bite, grows bitter at the second
and third chew. The pull of the past feels stronger as we grow
older, but it is the pull of death, for there is no permanence to
be had, not even in the long run, for death and taxes. As
William Blake puts it in his beautiful little poem "Eternity":

> He who binds to himself a joy
> Does the winged life destroy.

If we hug our happiness to ourselves, if we try to keep our children, our friends, our relationships, ourselves, our church, our politics, our institutions, our family life, as they now are, then one day we wake up to discover we're hugging a corpse —for "he who binds to himself a joy, does the winged life destroy."

We confuse duration with significance—as I was reminded recently at the funeral of the sixteen-year-old boy. The significance of his life is not to be measured in terms of its length, but in terms of the depth of his every day, the fullness, the totality, the wild, open abandon with which he gave himself, day by day, to his days. Duration in a marriage or a friendship can kill a sick relationship, or deepen a healthy relationship. Predictability in a person, in a relationship, in an institution, is boring. Sameness is death on a platter. For eternity is not linear, not endlessness stretching out ad infinitum, ad nauseam. Eternity is not permanence, but significance; not duration, but depth.

Or we confuse permanence with continuity. Permanence we cannot have, do not need, though we want it. Continuity we can have and do need, though we may or may not want it. As the journalist wrote:

> The winter solstice demonstrates again that undeniable universal rhythm which beats through the life and substance of everything we know. It is there in the atom, in the sunlight itself, in the color of the sunset. It is in the throbbing of the human heart, the crying of the winter wind, the progression of the seasons, the wheeling of the years. We live by it, beings of that rhythm in our very breath, in our speech, in our songs, in our birthing and loving and in our growing old . . . and the great rhythms beat through the least of us as through the universe.[1]

Even the smallest of creatures has a sun in its eyes.

The continuity of our throbbing life is not permanence, but newness, the constant regeneration of the universe as of its smallest creatures, galaxies and grasshoppers.

Artists are people like you and me who paint a picture or write a poem, or love a person, or make a new thing, or dream a dream about that newness that surges forth within us and sometimes overwhelms us. One such dreamer and hoper wrote:

> Then I saw a new heaven and a new earth. . . . I heard a loud voice proclaiming from the throne: "Now at last God has his dwelling among men! He will dwell among them and they shall be his people, and God himself will be with them. He will wipe every tear from their eyes; there shall be an end to death and to mourning and crying and pain; for the old order has passed away! . . . Behold, I am making all things new!" [2]

"I AM MAKING ALL THINGS NEW" is a long name, but it is one of the names of God. "I AM MAKING ALL THINGS NEW"—that's who he is. "I AM MAKING ALL THINGS NEW" is the truth about the nature of the universe and its smallest creatures. It may be the most adequate still photo of eternity that we can take. It's the bubbling nucleus of the dream. It's the aching hope in your heart and mind. With the death of permanence is the birth of newness. As Nietzsche put it: "Only where there are graves are there resurrections." Only as the old order dies can the new order be born. Only as the old me dies, can the new me, and you, be born.

Newness is not to be confused with novelty. Novelty is that which diverts but does not deepen. Novelties are properly to be found in five-and-dime stores. Newness is found in the blood, sweat, and tears of joy. Novelty fades away; newness is reborn again and again and again. "I AM MAKING ALL THINGS NEW" is one of the names of God. So:

> He who binds to himself a joy
> Does the winged life destroy;
> But he who kisses the joy as it flies
> Lives in eternity's sunrise.

Because God is making all things new; because newness and life, not permanence and death, are the twin engines of creation, we can embrace transience without fear and kiss the joy as it flies. Transience is the outside of newness, eternity is the inside; transience the dying flesh, eternity the living spirit. Transience says: Let us eat, drink, and be merry, for tomorrow we die. Eternity says: Let us love, give and be joyful, for today we live. William Blake somehow opens that door of eternity for us when he says:

> To see a world in a grain of sand
> And a heaven in a wild flower;
> Hold infinity in the palm of your hand,
> And eternity in an hour.[3]

Can you think of some hours in the last year or few weeks so bittersweet and beautiful that you knew, even in the living of them, that they were eternal, to abide forever in your memory and hope? "He who kisses the joy as it flies, lives in eternity's sunrise."

To kiss the joy as it flies is to live in the Spirit; it is to live boldly, immediately, with gracious abandon, daring to risk much, willing to give oneself. It is to live for a moment "in unison with our dream"; to see the sun shining in the eyes of the smallest creatures; to "create the marvelous by contagion." [4]

Have we been kissing the joy as it flies?

The other night, late, in our family room, one of our daughters was sitting with Peggy and me, talking casually. We don't often get special moments of communion with our kids, but this time we were listening to a new Judy Collins record called "Living" that someone had given us for Christmas. There's one song on the record that we all love and have heard so many times that we know it. So as we were listening, each of us on our own just started to sing along with Judy. Then there came a moment of singing delight when our eyes met and arms touched and voices merged, and we were together with our girl, kissing the joy as it flies.

In that same family room the night before Christmas, our boy, Bobby, was there. We have a fireplace in the family room, and the Christmas tree is in the living room. (I don't know why we have a living room because we do all our living in the family room!) But anyhow, Bobby and I were there and he was looking at the fireplace, and all of a sudden he turned to me, thunderstruck, with an urgent revelation which had just come to him. He said, "Daddy, Santa Claus is going to come down the chimney and he won't see any tree, and he's going to go without leaving the presents!" Well, this was a serious discovery that required immediate consultation, of course, as to what to do. Bobby got the idea that we should draw Santa Claus a map and show him exactly where to go, into the kitchen and through the hall and around to that important tree where he could leave those generous gifts he was going to bring. So a map was made and put on the fireplace hearth, and that night Bobby went to bed in peace and confidence. Later on, much later, I went to bed, kissing the joy as it flies.

A couple of weeks ago I came through the garage door to

hear two of our daughters shouting at each other angrily. I
heard one side fully because that girl was downstairs, and the
other upstairs. So, quickly, too quickly, hastily, I took her side,
went upstairs, angry myself, dealt harshly with my other
daughter and left her crying, and came back downstairs,
trembling myself—only to find out in a few more minutes of
conversation that I hadn't gotten the full story. The fault was
on both sides and I had done a gross injustice to one of my
daughters. Well, I don't know if this kind of thing happens
to you sometimes, but I just felt awful! I had blown it again!
But with this daughter, it was the first time I'd lost my temper and really exploded my anger. And, I figured, she's tough,
and she's just going to hold that in her heart, and she's not
going to forgive me for hours or for days. She's got a right to
be bitter—and Christmas was coming, and I'd really hurt her
feelings!

So after a while of just moping around, I went back up to
her room without much hope and knocked on her door,
expecting it to be locked and kept locked. But she said,
"Come in." There she was, sitting on the floor, crying.

I said, "Look, honey, I made a mistake and I'm wrong—forgive me."

Very quietly and readily, she said, "Daddy, I do forgive
you," and we were quiet there while I received her forgiveness.

Then through the evening I tried to do little things, like
bring her a cookie, or ask her what time it was—little tokens,
you know, because I was feeling sorry for what I'd done.
Until at one point I was standing again in her doorway and
she said, "Daddy, you don't have to do those things. I really
have forgiven you." Eternity in an hour, kissing the joy as it
flies.

Christmas Eve a little boy came up to me after one of the

services and gave me a prayer card on which he had written a message to me. It read: "Dear Dr. Raines, I hope you have a Merry Christmas and may the Angel of the Lord shine on to you." Well, the Angel of the Lord has been shining on to me through the heart of that little boy. I put that card up on my bulletin board in my study so I'll see it now and then.

The Angel of the Lord shone on you, didn't he, several times in the last week or two? A little note, a little gesture that someone gave to you that expressed the heart? Some little note that you wrote, really a self-love gift to someone? Eternity in an hour, kissing the joy as it flies.

A man in prison wrote me this week: "There's a high chain link fence below my second story window, and on the top of the fence there are huge coils of barbed wire. A dozen or so little sparrows were flitting about in the barbed wire, and they reminded me of that scriptural verse about God caring even for the sparrow that falls, so I wrote a little poem that I'd like to share with you." I'll share with you four out of the six stanzas, it may not be great poetry, but it is great faith and hope:

> My prison house is cold and grey
> and made of rock and steel,
> It's filled with tears both night and day,
> there's little love to feel.
>
> The sick and sad and broken men
> who suffer here with me
> Cannot recall the joys of when
> they last were gay and free.
>
> Yet I am happy and I'm free
> though tombed within this Hell,
> for Mighty Acts of God I see
> through cold bars of my cell.

> For sparrows play outside my wall,
> and flit from fence to tree.
> I know he grieves their every fall
> and he is here with me.[5]

Whatever prison you're in, he is there with you and me, when we fall, when we rise, making us new and beautiful in our time and setting us free . . .

> to taste eternity in an hour . . .
> to create the marvelous by contagion . . .
> to notice the butterflies when they come
>   and sit on our shoulder . . .
> to have the courage, sometimes, to live in unison
>   with our dream . . .
> and the hope, always, to kiss the joy as it flies.

You Can
Choose to Be Real

ONE OF the men I admire most in the world today is Alexander Solzhenitsyn, the Russian author. He was recently denied the reception of the Nobel Prize by his government because he had publicly decried the suppression of liberty in the Soviet Union. During the Stalin regime, he wrote a letter to a friend in which he criticized Stalin, for which "crime" he spent eight years in a prison camp. Then a few more years were spent in the cancer ward of a hospital. His writing comes out of his living. He is a man who is what he says, does what he is, and lives what he believes.

What is moving and impressive to me about Solzhenitsyn is that the pressures of his imprisonment, sickness, deprivation, personal attacks, loneliness, and the loss of nearly everything precious to him, distilled all the triviality and superficiality away so that what finally emerged from that furnace of pressure was the hard polished jewel of his essential humanity. All that deprivation forged him into a truly free human being. Solzhenitsyn has one of his characters in prison say:

> "The happiness of incessant victory, the happiness of fulfilled desire, the happiness of success and of total satiety—*that* is suffering! That is spiritual death. . . . [People] waste themselves in senseless thrashing around for the sake of a handful of goods and die without realizing their spiritual wealth. . . .[1] It is not our level of prosperity that makes for happiness but the kinship of heart to heart and the way we look at the world. Both attitudes lie within our power, so that a man is happy so long as he chooses to be happy, and no one can stop him." [2]

We could argue with Solzhenitsyn's thesis that happiness does not consist in external favorable circumstances but in that inner citadel of freedom of choice, because sometimes those external pressures destroy us. But let's listen to what he is trying to say. He is trying to say that you and I can choose our attitude, whatever our circumstances are—that we can choose to be happy, not in the sense of contentment, but in the sense of integrity. What matters is not what becomes of you but what you become. You determine that. You and I decide what we will be. As Solzhenitsyn puts it, "Everyone forges his inner self year after year. One must try to cut, to polish one's soul so as to become a human being." [3] Souls bleed when they get cut. Souls are seared in the process. Sometimes we have to be burned in order to become beautiful. And there is a difference between liberty and freedom. Liberty is external and can be given to us or taken away from us—but freedom is that inner citadel of choice which is always ours.

For me, this inner freedom, this independence, means that

I can't waste much time on self-pity. I can't waste much time or energy bemoaning my fate, complaining about the past, blaming my parents or my kids or wife or circumstances or anything for who I am. If there are contradictions in me, it is because I allow them to be there, to stay there. I am responsible for who I am. If there are coercions, I will never be free of them because life consists of coercions, whether in a job or marriage or circumstances. As Viktor Frankl said of his death camp experience, "Everything can be taken from a man but one thing: the last of the human freedoms—to choose one's attitude in any given set of circumstances." [4]

But I can choose how to express my creativity in the context of the circumstances that coerce me, in the confidence that real spiritual freedom is like a plant pushing up through the cement that one day will break that cement into pieces. Independence for me means freedom and responsibility to decide who I will be and to choose in my circumstances to be real. What would it mean for you, right now, today, to make a *declaration of independence* in your life and circumstances? What would it mean for you to decide who you will be, to take full responsibility for who you are and to choose to be real?

A new *independence* and a new *interdependence*. If it is good for us to stand alone, it is also good for us to stand together. My own need for interdependence broke through to me with fear and pain the other night. I came home late. I was badly upset by an experience that had frightened me, an experience of physical terror such as I had not felt for years. I narrowly escaped being physically beaten, and perhaps maimed or killed. When I came home, my teeth were chattering. Peggy was out of town. One of my daughters happened to be up. I had to talk to somebody so I started talking to her and just poured it all out. She was great. She nodded, she understood. She made me some soup and grilled cheese sandwiches, and we talked together for more than an hour. At some point during that time, I realized that I was out of my father/parent authority role with her and that, for a little while, we were there together as human being to human being. It was really mutual, person to person. I felt a tremendous gratitude to her because she was helping me in one of those times when I knew I needed to be helped and understood. I don't know what difference that may make in our relationship in the future, but for me that was a revelatory moment with implications for all of my relationships.

More than I yet realize, I grew up thinking, "There are strong people and weak people, and I'm one of the strong ones." Strong people are supposed to give to other people's needs and not to have any needs, or very few, themselves. This subtle falsehood was further wrapped around me in the clergy role I adopted, which sanctified and professionalized this idea: "You need me, but I don't need you." I believe that many people who exercise power or authority, people with charisma, people in the helping professions, are subject to this falsehood. Such people (maybe including you) typically identify with their strengths and ignore or are unaware of their weaknesses and needs.

In my fear the other night, I realized afresh that every person is both strong and weak; that in every strength there is a corroding weakness and in every weakness there is an enriching strength. Every one of us needs to receive as well as to give. Any human relationship can be a mutual exchange, whatever the differences in age, in power, in sex. Indeed, only when a relationship in some fashion is mutual, is it not degrading for those who participate in it. So if you view yourself as essentially strong, then you need to discover, to acknowledge and express your weakness, to know where and when you are vulnerable, when you need comfort and encouragement. Someone said, "The Lord loves a cheerful receiver." Only when we can acknowledge our needs do others feel free to give us their love because otherwise they feel we don't need it or want it, and they are shy then to offer their gifts. Only when we are aware of our own yearning, our own emptiness, are we able to reveal ourselves to another person. The door that has *need* on one side of it has *self-revelation* on the other side. Unless we can get that *need* door open, we aren't going to be able to give ourselves to people, to tell them who we are. I've been thinking recently how few people there are to whom I reveal myself, my inner self, how few people there are, therefore, who really know me. There is something a little sad in that for me, but something appropriate, too. There is an appropriateness for self-revelation, a time and a place. However, much of the time I keep my doors closed out of fear and pride.

How is it with you? To whom do you reveal yourself? Who really knows you? If we view ourselves as essentially weak or damaged, then we need to discover and experience and acknowledge and express our own strength. It is there. Every adolescent who would break out of his cocoon has to go this way. Every person whose self-esteem has been damaged must go this way.

Some prisoners from the Ohio penitentiary have participated in a growth group in our church recently. There is a reality about them that facilitates cutting through façades that prevent people from seeing each other. At the final meeting of one of these groups, a prisoner who had been in the group for twelve weeks held up a big piece of paper on which he had written, "Twelve weeks ago I thought of myself as a convict. Today I think of myself as a human being," and in large letters under it, "Thank you all."

Do you have friends or a group with whom you can rediscover your own humanity and know for sure that however you may be damaged or may have damaged another, still you are a human being, you belong to the family?

The Women's Liberation movement, which is spreading across the world and across my breakfast table, begins with the insistence that there is no weaker sex, and I'll grant that one right off! It is also an insistence on genuine equality of relationship, a movement away from unhealthy dependence to a healthy interdependence. The Women's Liberation movement is going to affect our lives more profoundly than some of the more dramatic liberation movements of these days. In education, employment, politics, religion and many other areas, as women's self-perceptions change, men's self-perceptions will also have to change. Marriage will become more problematic and more promising. The man/woman relationship in and out of marriage will become more open, more honest, more fascinating, more risky, more significant.

Sisters and brothers, it is happening! I mean, you should see the books appearing in our house these days. Coffee table, kitchen table, bedroom, bathroom—the titles of these books: *Sexual Politics*; *The Female Eunuch*; *The American Woman, Who Was She?*; *Sisterhood Is Powerful*; *Gentlemen Prefer Slaves*. I'm learning what it means to be a pig—guinea pig, male chauvinist pig! Recently I went up to a woman in our congregation who keeps pushing me about why there aren't more women on our staff (she has a point) and said, "Hello, your favorite male chauvinist pig reporting." She looked at me with mingled pity and sympathy and said, "Bob, I don't think you are a male chauvinist pig. I think you are an old-fashioned hypocrite." What a put-down! She was saying that when it comes to women's liberation, I talk a good game but don't do anything about it. It's like race relations. We're all in favor of equality and justice and so on, but . . . "Don't move in next door to me" . . . "Don't show up across my breakfast table."

What would it mean for you in your marriage, your family, your friendships, your relationships at work, to make a *declaration of interdependence*, really to see the other person, to come through the role and function and engage that other person as human being to human being? That is hard to do. It has to be done day by day. We pigeonhole the people we live and work with most closely. We impale them on the bulletin boards of our imagination and say, "She is like that," or "He is like this." We eliminate the possibility of surprise, kill spontaneity, and look to others for something new under the sun. We cannot deny our functions or our roles because we are structured the way we are. We are spouses, we are fathers, parents and children and colleagues. But we can try to see each other real.

In the play *The Rainmaker*, Lizzie, the daughter, tells a friend about her father:

"Some nights I'm in the kitchen washing the dishes. And Pop's playing poker with the boys. Well, I'll watch him real close. And at first I'll just see an ordinary middle-aged man—not very interesting to look at. And then, minute by minute, I'll see little things I never saw in him before. Good things and bad things—queer little habits I never noticed he had—and ways of talking I never paid any mind to. And suddenly I know who he is—and I love him so much I could cry! I want to thank God I took the time to see him real." [5]

You and I can choose to see and be real.

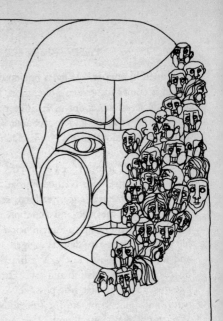

My Name Is Mob

Nᴏᴛ ʟᴏɴɢ ago I was trying to catch the subway in New York City, rushed down the stairs, across the platform, heard the screech of the oncoming train, got in the middle of the milling crowd, pushed and shoved my way just through the doors before they closed, crammed into a window seat and looked at that mob, pushing, jamming, shoving, the neon light of the newsstands, a kind of jungle out there. There was a lurch and all of a sudden as I looked out that window, I saw myself, my own face, in the dark of the tunnel, reflected back at me, eyes staring. Uncomfortable, silent, meeting of myself in the dark.

That subway encounter of myself came to my mind as I have been pondering the story of the madman in the gospel. In the presence of Jesus, he suddenly came to himself. Jesus saw him, and asked him, "What is your name?" And he answered, "My name is Mob; for there are so many of us in me." [1] This man saw himself in the eyes of Jesus and, like a blurred slide being brought into focus, his image suddenly popped up clearly before him—there it was, quiet, together.

I have been pondering that question for myself. What is your name? My name is Mob. There are so many of us in me, such chaotic, raw vitality. What is your name? Is there a mob in you, too? Will you explore with me out of your own inner struggle two questions that plague me?

The first is, *how can my power of being be creative rather than destructive?* There is a mob in you and me as in the madman story and the mob is violent, pregnant with surges of power that can explode in chaotic destructiveness or can turn into imagination, creativity, love. The mob in you and in me will always be poised with potential for grandeur and misery. When did you first begin to realize or experience the destructive powers of your being? Remember?

Well, my mob broke loose on a job in Philadelphia, an urban church in decline that needed all the strength that could be gathered on a small staff. So I thought when I got there, get a strong man, as strong as possible, to join me in a co-ministry where we could share power, responsibility, and everything along down the line. I was so naïve that I didn't realize that I could be threatened by anybody. I was so naïve that I was unaware of the kinds of severe tensions that such an anti-nature structure, what some people called the two-headed monster, would put us through.

Ted Loder and I worked and lived in that structure for eight years. For the congregation, it was a productive and dynamic structure, with some tension. For Ted and me, it was a furnace of personal struggle, pain, confrontation, and growth. Ted knew himself a lot better than I knew myself. At first I refused to give him the satisfaction of losing my temper. I was beyond that. I would not spill my guts on the table—until one day the anger in me exploded with such force that suddenly I found myself uncontrollably in a furious rage which left me shaking, appalled at the violent powers within me of which I had been unaware all those years. Ted had pulled the cork on my negative feelings, which I realize now had been building up since childhood. Then I had learned to hold them in, restrain them, keep them in control. I discovered in that experience, and in many that followed, a range and depth of hostility that was frightening because I couldn't always control it any more. But at the same time there was released out of me more sheer power of being, more vitality, more raw energy than had yet appeared. Some part of me had been under wraps. For better or for worse, more of me came exploding into the world.

So how is it with you? Have you had moments or occasions or events like that when you got in touch with your destructive potentiality? When the mob in you broke loose for awhile? Maybe it happens on the job with the pressures you have been feeling from the boss or a colleague. Or maybe at home. It is so often the tiny little things that push you over the edge. Over the years it has been building, or over the days of that week, and then it gets to you. Maybe it is that way your spouse coughs, or that certain gesture or glance that just drives you batty. The anger pours out in language and behavior that you just don't believe. And the pretty, polished surface of the relationship is cracked into pieces. Maybe we really shouldn't be surprised when all the hell in us breaks out at home because that is partly what home is for, home and church.

One time the mother of a teen-aged daughter, when her daughter had said and done some extraordinarily mean things, said to her, "How hostile and mean you are. Every word that comes out of your mouth is venomous. How do they stand you at school?" To which her daughter replied, "You don't know me. I am a different person at school. All day long I have to hold in my feelings, but at home I can let all my frustrations out."

Home is meant to be a place where our destructive energies may be exploded in the hope that the covenant and commitment are strong enough to sustain whatever chaos and cruelty come out. Church is meant to be a place where all of our madmen and madwomen with all their destructive potential can let it hang out in hope that there is strength and grace among us sufficient to heal any hurt, to quell any violence, and to help us put it back together. We all need people who are able to receive all of you and me, and especially that part of us we are afraid won't be accepted. We need people who understand, who are there, who are available, who are around, who are ready with arms, hearts, hope, and stability to help us get it together again.

I am inclined to offer a cautionary note here. We can deify the expression of anger. We are obviously living in a time, culturally, when anger is in; courtesy and restraint are out. Expressions of anger are not always appropriate or creative. In an article some time ago in *Time* magazine entitled "Look Back on Anger," Melvin Maddocks writes:

Anger is the emotion we tend to feel when in doubt about what else we feel. Anger . . . today is becoming one of our most praised values. In raising anger to an emotional ideal, we have gravely misgauged the limited utility of adrenalin's quick flashes. In art, anger is regularly mistaken for sincerity,

if not inspiration. . . . Anger of any kind has also become
the accepted proof of moral conviction. It is the way we act
out of certainty when we do not really feel it. . . . Even love,
itself, can become a junior partner. What fierce, cannibalistic
love scenes we stage in films and even in private lives! Such
*Who's Afraid of Virignia Woolf*ishness! Such ripping and
tearing! Such savage, winner-takes-all grappling! . . . In *The
Intimate Enemy*, Dr. George R. Bach, a clinical psychologist,
turns anger into an art, or possibly a science. . . . "Anger,"
Dr. Bach concludes, "cannot be dishonest." Upon Bach's
misapprehension, America's newest industry, group therapy,
founders. Venting hostility is so simplistically scripted as the
"Moment of Truth" that a whole cult of anger fakers has
developed, not unlike the faith fakers who also deceived
themselves into salvation at other and earlier camp meetings.
Anger ought to be an alarm system that warns us of our
deepest concerns. But left to itself, it can become an undis-
criminating rant, equalizing the serious and the trivial, the
horrors of Biafra and the poor quality of frozen dinners. . . .
We can refuse to glamorize it when it is self-indulgence, the
sound of baby shoes stamping. . . .[2]

I value encounter groups, and affirm the idea of letting it
all hang out. But there is always the question of what is appropriate. Sometimes when I let all my anger out, it may
give me momentary relief but it may destroy someone else.
Sometimes I should hold my anger in for the sake of another.

What is your name? Is the mob in you still bottled up or
locked away somewhere with the key thrown away? It does
seem safer that way, more orderly that way. You don't get
into as much trouble and not as much risk or jeopardy—even
if half of you never sees the light of day—even if you live
on four cylinders and never discover that you are an eight
cylinder person.

That time when I lost control of my feelings in an

encounter group and was overwhelmed with an onslaught of sobbing, the first thing that rolled out of me was resentment. Resentment toward God, my parents, church, binding me into feelings of excessive responsibility. But those resentment feelings were followed immediately by appreciation feelings, appreciation for God, my parents, for the church. I realized literally in my own body that the creative and destructive powers of my being flow out of the same depth. I know that I don't want to stifle or muffle or smother my vitality. I want it to flow out in creative, responsible, loving ways in the confidence that the deepest power in me is not dark but light, healthy, good; and that I can trust my own depths and learn to let me out with all the attendant risks and mistakes, growing into the experience of my full being including the madness in me, the beautiful madness.

Everybody has a little madness. We can celebrate our madness. Sam Keen, in a book called *To a Dancing God*, writes:*

> God, but I want madness!
> I want to tremble,
> to be shaken,
> to yield to pulsation,
> to surrender to the rhythm of music and sea,
> to the seasons of ebb and flow,
> to the tidal surge of love.
>
> I am tired of being
> hard,
> tight,
> controlled,
> tensed against the invasion of novelty,
> armed against tenderness,
> afraid of softness.

* Abridged from pp. 117-20 in *To A Dancing God* by Sam Keen. Copyright © 1970 by Sam Keen. By permission of Harper & Row, Publishers, Inc.

I am tired of
directing my world,
making,
doing,
shaping.

Tension is ecstasy in chains.
The muscles are tightened to prevent trembling.
Nerves strain to prevent trust, hope, relaxation.

Surrendering,
giving in to the involuntary is:
madness (idiots tremble),
ecstasy (being out of my skin, what am I?),
bliss (love is coming together and parting),
grace (dancing with the whole spirit).

. . . .

God, give me madness
that does not destroy
wisdom,
responsibility,
love.[3]

That is a prayer I can pray with my whole heart, and may-be you can, too. God is in your madness and mine. He is in whatever you are afraid of, seeking always to make it creative, joyous, delightful, exuberant, wise, tender.

A few months after I left Philadelphia, I got a letter from my former colleague, Ted Loder. When we parted, our relationship was amiable, wary, blocked. I had not written Ted and I don't know when I would have, but he wrote me. He said among other things, "I feel that the anger, the hostility, the competitiveness and envy which we could never deal with or work through, kept the love and gratitude and respect from blooming full. Perhaps one doesn't get to the valley of love or the mountaintop of gladness until he crosses the desert of anger and resentment and fear. I guess I shall always regret that we got lost in the desert somehow, though even that may have been a gracious experience in that we may have grown wiser and learned something about ourselves in it. And God, I believe, did have mercy on us!"

God did have mercy on Ted and me and gave us better than we could have deserved or hoped. For us, the structure had to be changed before we could fully appreciate the humanity in one another. Sometimes in a marriage or in a job context or in the home with parents or kids, the structure has to be changed before we are released really to love each other without fear or resentment—though sometimes *we* can change so that, within the same structure, new possibilities can flourish.

Perhaps it is safe to let your destructive feelings begin to flow out in the presence of the spirit of Jesus, who can take you and me and deal with us. Maybe your madness can be healed and exalted, and the powers of your being, your passions, made tender and constructive.

A second question: *How can I, who am in pieces, get myself together?* Maybe it is on the job that a man or a woman feels torn to pieces, crammed into a pigeonhole, a cog in someone else's machine. Someone writes:

The fellows up in Personnel—they have a set of cards on me;
sprinkled perforations tell them my individuality . . .
And what am I? I am a chart on the cards of IBM.
The secret places of the heart have little secrecy for them.
It matters not how much I prate . . .
They punch with punishment the scroll;
the files are masters of my fate.
They are captains of my soul.

Maybe it is the role fragmentation that bugs you—having to be mother, wife, daughter, lover, friend, church member, citizen, person. For me, the change of role through the day, through the week, is a relief and a complementary enrichment and possibility. For me, the split is deeper than that of roles—those many me's inside competing for attention and allegiance.

Remember the medieval torturing method called quartering? A man's arms and legs were tied to four different horses and when the word was given, they galloped off in four different directions and the person was literally quartered, torn into pieces. At times I feel like that, the four me's in me—I want, I ought, I need, I love—going in four different directions, or two in one direction, two in another.

I remember years ago hearing the great black blues singer Billie Holiday singing in a bar on East 52nd Street in New York City where the best jazz used to be in the late '40s. One of the songs she sang was "All of me . . . take all of me." She had enormous charisma, an immense capacity to give herself in her singing. This week I remembered that phrase with envy and wonder—"all of me." When is "all of me"? When am I all together in one piece? Who can put the pieces of this Humpty Dumpty back together again? Not all the king's horses nor all the king's men, but maybe Jesus could if we were able to be quiet before him.

Sam Keen writes a little essay for Zorba the Greek:

> I long to release the gypsy in me who would roam the earth, tasting, sampling, traveling light. There are so many lives I want to live, so many styles I want to inhabit. In me sleeps Zorba's concern to allow no lonely woman to remain comfortless (Here am I, Lord—send me!), Camus's passion to lessen the sufferings of the innocent, Hemingway's drive to live

and write with lucidity, and the unheroic desire to see each day end with tranquillity and a shared cup of tea. I am so many, yet I may be only one. I mourn for all the selves I kill when I decide to be a single person. Decision is a cutting off. . . . I travel one path only by neglecting many. . . . So I turn my back on small villages I will never see, strange flesh I will not touch, ills I will not cure, and I choose to be in the world as a husband, a father, an explorer of ideas and styles of life. Perhaps Zorba will not leave me altogether. I would not like to live without dancing, without unknown roads to explore.[4]

Nor would I. Nor would you. Some of the me's in me may have to die before I can live. I don't know; I keep hoping not. I keep hoping that there is some way that the many-ness of me may be released into a unity that can thrive wisely.

What about you? How is it with you and your many you's and your longing to be a single person? A man writes, "I believe that everything wants a living place—its home, if you will, where it becomes what its essence is at a certain time and in a certain place. For example, a man who rests his case for life upon a sounding place, a spot on which his life can stand and from which he can say, 'Here the trembling stops.' "

Where does the trembling stop for you? With whom? Treasure those moments, rare perhaps, moments of peace, silent wonder, communion, joy. Moments, times, places where for you the trembling stops. Moments when the mob in you becomes a community. Moments when you are quiet, together. Like maybe . . . now.

Struggle
in the Dark

IN HARPER Lee's novel *To Kill a Mockingbird*, Atticus, wise
and generous man, tells his son, Jem, about an old woman who
is dying of cancer. Her name is Mrs. Dubose. She has been a
bitter critic of Atticus for his insistence on equal rights for
blacks in that small Southern town. So Jem hates the old
woman for criticizing his father. But Atticus wants his son to
see the greatness in this cantankerous old woman. For years
she had taken morphine, at her doctor's orders, to ease her
pain; eventually she became a morphine addict. As it became
clear that her days were numbered, she became determined to
end her addiction to morphine before she died so that she
would die beholden to nothing, to nobody. Jem reads to her
and watches her day by day as she endures the pain of not taking the morphine. After her death, Atticus says to Jem: "I

wanted you to see what real courage is, instead of getting the idea that courage is a man with a gun in his hand. It's when you know you're licked before you begin but you begin anyway and you see it through no matter what. You rarely win, but sometimes you do. Mrs. Dubose won, all ninety-eight pounds of her. According to her views, she died beholden to nothing and nobody. She was the bravest person I ever knew." [1]

Courage is struggling in the dark alone. Jacob found himself struggling in the dark alone. "And Jacob was left alone; and a man wrestled with him until the breaking of the day." [2] And what of you and me? Do you know what it is to be overtaken by some strange power and find yourself contending for you know not what except that the stakes are high? To what or to whom are you addicted? What sweet but enslaving power has its grip on you? Are you locked in some struggle where you live or work, a new calling, an old emptiness, a yearning?

Courage is struggling in the dark alone. Our deepest inner battles have to be fought alone. Our most important decisions have to be made alone. Our most painful uncertainties and sorrows have to be suffered alone.

A man died. His son was caught up in guilt and grief and relief that spiraled down into a depression—no chance to repair the relationship which had been broken. Chances had come in the recent months before the death and he had turned them down, and now there was no chance any more. Death ends a life but not a relationship. His son was struggling in the dark with his guilt, seeking in his remorse some sort of acceptance into the future. Are we struggling in the dark of some remorse towards acceptance into the future?

In John Updike's novel *Rabbit Redux*, Janice and Harry, a

couple in their thirties, were drifting along a joyless plateau, romance gone, curiosity in each other dead, spontaneity killed. They had become locked rooms to each other. They could hear each other cry but they couldn't get in. Are you locked up in some cold room in your marriage, your family, some friendship? Sometimes it is easy to wind along a joyless road year after year, never engaging each other face to face. Sometimes it is easier than to ask the painful questions, to risk the blood, sweat and tears, to admit that something has died and ask if it can live again. Janice, with unrighteous courage, strikes out for life, life with someone else, and gives the key to her locked room to another man. Are you struggling from some dark discontent toward vitality, beauty, and ambiguity?

Asher Lev, a twelve-year-old Jewish boy in Chaim Potok's novel *My Name Is Asher Lev*, longs to be a painter, and he pursues this longing in the face of his father's disapproval. His father is an orthodox Hasidic Jew. He wants his boy to be a scholar of the Torah, a rabbi maybe, or at least a doctor, lawyer, or successful businessman, but not a painter. Jewish sons do not become painters. His mother recognizes the torture and glory of his gift, his destiny, but is torn between her son and her husband. Young Asher persists on his quest despite the growing alienation from his parents. One time his guide and teacher says to him: "Art is whether or not there is a scream in [you] wanting to get out in a special way. . . . Or a laugh. Picasso laughs, too." [3] Is there a scream in you or a laugh, or an ache, that wants to get out in a special way, your way, your chosen way, the way of your inner leading? Do you long to be the artist of your own life and to paint the portrait of your own future? Will you pursue your own inner demands even though those close to you may be offended and misunderstand and try to deter you? Will you fight for your identity, vocation, your inner sense of who you are called to be? *Courage is struggling in the dark alone.*

Jacob had courage. In some ways he was a mean man. He was a selfish man. He took advantage of people. He used his strength to gain advantage. But he had courage. He had the courage to exert all the power of his being to defeat the unknown assailant. Courage to wring some blessing out of that cursed struggle. His assailant said: "Let me go . . ." Jacob said: "I will not let you go unless you bless me." The assailant said: "What is your name?" Jacob: "Jacob." The assailant: "Your name shall no more be called Jacob, but Israel [which means he who strives with God] for you have striven with God and with men and have prevailed . . ." [4]

The assailant that struggles with you and me in the dark may be God. It may be he who is struggling with you in your remorse, discontent, aching, getting to you where you are most alive. What matters is that you and I refuse to give up or let go, that we hold on with all the tenacity of our being to seize what beauty there may be in the terror; what meaning in the chaos. What matters is that we insist on pursuing our own inner destiny despite the conventional cost. We may be wrong—we often are—and the pain and the hurt may seem to outweigh the fulfillment wrung out. of existence. And we can never know ahead of time. We can only determine to engage that assailant in the dark and to throw everything we are and have into the struggle in hope that in the depth of that darkness, the heart of that chaos, we will meet God face to face.

Updike has a character say: "There is a steady state, and though it is true everything is expanding outwards, it does not thin out to . . . nothingness . . . [because] through strange holes in this nothingness new somethingness comes pouring in from exactly nowhere . . . men do beautiful things in that mud. It is where God is pushing through. . . . Chaos is his Holy face . . ." [5] Stare into the chaos until you see his face. Squeeze the emptiness within you until it fills up. Pin your darkness to the ground until light breaks forth from caves. Let your guilt and grief and discontent drive nails into your hands and heart, holes through which the grace of God may come.

Rilke wrote finally:

> At bottom the only courage that is demanded of us; to have courage for the most strange, the most singular and the most inexplicable that we may encounter . . . for it is not inertia alone that is responsible for human relationships repeating themselves from case to case, indescribably monotonous and unrenewed; it is shyness before any sort of new, unforesee-able experience with which one does not think one's self able to cope. But only someone who is ready for everything, who excludes nothing, not even the most enigmatical, will live the relation to another as something alive and will him-self draw exhaustively from his own existence. For if we think of this existence of the individual as a larger or smaller room, it appears evident that most people learn to know only a corner of their room, a place by the window, a strip of floor on which they walk up and down. Thus they have a certain security. And yet that dangerous insecurity is so much more human which drives the prisoners in Poe's stories to feel out the shapes of their horrible dungeons and not be strangers to the unspeakable terror of their abode.[6]

Courage is struggling in the dangerous insecurity alone. It is seeking beauty in the terror and joy in the pain. It is hanging on until you are blessed and given a new name.

Jacob was named and lamed. His assailant touched him on

the thigh and left him limping in the daylight. If you and I are named by God, we will also be lamed by God, scarred with some mark of meaning, some thorn in the flesh which we will carry with us all our days to remind us that we have been touched by God. God leaves holes, nail holes in our hands and hearts through which his grace can keep pouring in to heal whom he has hurt. To be touched by God is not to avoid suffering. It is to be drawn or driven into your own authentic suffering, that suffering that is central to your own being and becoming, in the suffering of which you go limping in the daylight.

Harry looks at his wife, Janice, who is seeking life and love somewhere else. He thinks to himself: "Growth is betrayal. There is no other route. There is no arriving somewhere without leaving somewhere." [7]

Growth is betrayal of arrangements that were . . .

Growth is change that is threatening as well as promising . . .

Growth is denial of something and affirmation of something else . . .

Growth is dangerous and glorious insecurity . . .

Are you growing on your way? Are you limping in the daylight?

Mary Main is. She is sixty-seven years old, blind. She lives in Provincetown, Massachusetts. She is a writer and lives alone. She said to someone recently: "Of course I get depressed. . . . Don't you? But depression isn't as painful as it was before. I'm aware of my limitations. . . . When people discuss paintings, I don't try to join in. I've learned to accept blindness. . . . Before I became blind, I thought blind people saw only blackness. . . . But when I wake at night it sometimes seems to me that the room is bright, bright. I often go to feel

if the light is switched on. If I say to myself at night, 'I remember blue skies—think blue! Blue, blue, do I see blue.' I
touch a delphinium and I see blue. I dream in color all the
time. I'm always blind in my dreams, but I see. I get angry
because I lose my cane, but I see, I see." [8]

> O Lord, we are struggling in the dark
> But we see, we see—
> We dream in color and imagine
> That we are free, free—
> You have touched us, O Lord, and it hurts . . .
> You have blessed us, O Lord, and it heals . . .
> As you have given us courage
> To struggle in the dark alone
> Give us courage now
> To go limping in the daylight together.

The
Yearning Gap

AMERICAN LIFE has been filled with gaps in recent years
—the credibility gap, the dollar gap, the missile gap, the learning gap. There is another gap deep inside you and in me and
between us which we may call the yearning gap. Paul acknowledged his yearning for his dear friends in Philippi when
he wrote them from prison in Rome, "I hold you in my heart,
for you are all partakers with me of grace. . . . I yearn for
you all with the affection of Christ Jesus." [1]

What does our yearning feel like? Yearning rises out of
distance and depth. We yearn for those we can't quite touch,
reach, possess, understand, communicate with as we long to
do. We suffer the limits of our circumstances, our health,
choices already made, the limits of our capacity to understand
and be understood. We yearn out of precious memory to-

ward eager hope or perhaps fond remembrances of things past that are not to come again. Our deepest feeling toward God, toward one another and ourselves is alive in our yearning, which is a kind of soaring prayer. We can say that the quintessence of being alive is to feel our own yearning and understand it and share it with someone else. It is also to understand another's yearning and to share his yearning, too. What are the distance and depth of our yearning?

There is the yearning of adolescence, of youth, a yearning toward identity and independence, a yearning to find someone to love and be loved by. There is a yearning to taste and touch and smell and see and hear all of life, to experience everything at least once. There is a yearning to explore the farthest corners of the world in human experience, to probe into the deepest sources of our own being.

The other night we took our three daughters to a concert at St. John's Arena at Ohio State University to hear the British musician Elton John. The place was packed with thousands of young people. This man was superb at the piano, a kind of combination of barrelhouse, blues, and rock. He was a showman with syncopated rhythm and delicious chording. He had the whole place rocking and people clapping like a congregation at a camp meeting—total participation and involvement, exhausting and exhilarating. Everybody got caught up in it. I looked sideways at our three girls and saw their faces, radiant and alive. They were shaking, rocking, clapping, dancing. We exchanged grins and, for a moment, we were together in a kind of common yearning. It was really their yearning they were letting me tune in on—one of those special moments when you are together for a little while. We don't experience the depth of the family often, but it needs to happen once in a while so we stay in touch with one another's yearning. Music does it for us sometimes, maybe for you, too. Maybe it happens with sports or picnics or whatever your family does to have some moments together when you share one another's yearning.

Are you listening to the yearning of your kids? Is there some time in your day or week when they can tell you about that wonderful girl or guy they met, or about flunking that test, about getting hurt so badly, about a dream they dreamed, what they believe and hope? Do we take time and energy and love enough to share their yearning?

There is also the yearning of middlescence, middle age, which seeps forth, leaps forth, or breaks open in the late thirties or early forties. You wake up some day and you look in the mirror and are appalled to realize who you've become. You realize, like Zorba, you have a wife, kids, house, mortgage, the whole catastrophe! You ask yourself, "Is this what it's all about? Is there anything more? Is it downhill from now on?"

You may have seen the cartoon of the dejected looking man sitting on a bar stool looking hopelessly at the bartender. The bartender is leaning over the bar and saying, "OK, so you are forty. You've lived half your life. Look at the bright side. If you were a horse, you would already be dead fifteen years."

Time magazine, in an article some years ago about the perils and promise of middle age, painted some of the bright side and gave us some bon mots to comfort us a little. *Time* says that the fascination of a middle-aged woman is

> the distillation of glamor into poise, inner amusement and enriched femininity that no twenty-year-old sex kitten has lived long enough to acquire. . . . The young laugh at the way things seem; middle age laughs at the way things are. The young want to dynamite the treasure vaults of life; mid-

dle age has learned the combination. The young think they
know; middle age knows that no one knows. . . . Before
forty, one adds and feeds to gorge the ego; after forty, one
subtracts and simplifies to feed the soul.[2]

I was doing all right until I came to that last sentence because that doesn't ring true for me: "After forty, one subtracts and simplifies to feed the soul." Maybe that's the way it
ought to be and perhaps it is that way for you. But my experience of the forties is addition, not subtraction; rather than
simplification, more complexity inside me and around me in
my relationships. Middle age carries the major burden of society for family and public responsibility. There is a major
complexity of relationships, of relating to the older generation
and to the younger generation even as we try to figure out the
changes and the dynamics fermenting within us. To ask the
question seriously, "Who will I choose to be for the next
twenty or thirty years of my creative, productive life?" is to
start an earthquake inside you and around you in such a way
that the ground of your being and yearning will never again
be the same.

A fascinating article appeared in the May 1972 issue of
Psychology Today entitled "Multiple Identity—The Healthy,
Happy Human Being Wears Many Masks." It suggests that
the familiar idea of a basic-core self deep inside, that wears
many masks and expresses itself and hides itself in different
ways, is inaccurate. Instead, the article suggests, we are made
up of multiple selves. As our experiences and relationships
grow and come into newness, new selves are called out of us
and we meet people inside us whom we had not met before.
The healthy person is the person who acknowledges and
owns all his selves, decides which ones to neglect and kill

and which ones to nourish and foster. He is a person who finally embraces all his identity in hope.[3]

This multiple self-concept is more real to me in my own experience of middle age. There are strange inner yearnings calling me this way and that, and sometimes they are in conflict with one another.

The staff of our church had a two-day retreat recently. We were seeking to grow in our interpersonal and interprofessional relationships. At one point, the trainer instructed us to write on a large piece of paper words that expressed our feelings about ourselves at that time. We were then to pin the paper on our chests and walk around the room and see what other people had written and discuss it. I walked around and looked and noted until I was struck by a word on the chest of a man whom I supposed to have it all together. Quiet, confident, whole, peaceful, yet he had written on his paper the word *contradictory*. We smiled, like brothers, because I had also written the word *contradictory*. It is surprising to find our yearning threatening as well as promising. Instead of a neat, tidy, precise order within, there may be centrifugal, random, chaotic surges of being, more power of being than peace of mind.

Walt Whitman once wrote, "Do I contradict myself? Very well then, I contradict myself. (I am large, I contain multitudes.)"[4] So do you and so do I. Sometimes those inner multitudes are like a mob and sometimes like a community. They make things messy and marvelous. Is it possible that God is in our deepest yearnings, in the heart of our contradictions, calling us forth to love him with all our yearning, so that we may be able to love each other and ourselves wisely and joyously?

There is also the yearning of elderescence, of old age. Swiss author Georges Simenon began to feel old when he was fifty-seven. He began to experience self-doubts and to wonder if his life had any value, if anyone would remember him. Who would remember him? Who would miss him? He began to keep diaries of his feelings during that period of time. Over a period of two years he experienced the crisis of moving into old age and then, suddenly, he was through it and beyond it and moving into a very creative, satisfying time of his life.

He published the diaries ten years later under the title *When I Was Old*.[5] As I read the book, I began to realize there must be something like a crisis of elderescence. It comes in the fifties or sixties or seventies or whenever one realizes, "I'm old, really and honestly, no matter how young I feel. I'm old." Like the crisis of middlescence, like the crisis of adolescence, one comes to a new picture of himself and his prospects in the situation.

There were expressions of Simenon's longings to be reassured that he was somebody, that he mattered, that his life had been useful. There was a need to be recognized and honored. He wanted his children to know him in his vulnerability—to understand that he had self-doubts and fears and feelings, that he was a man of many sins. He wanted them to know him as he really was and understand that they might be better human beings than he was. He found himself less sure of himself and sometimes feeling like a stranger in a world that began to feel alien and remote to him.

I can identify with some of these feelings myself, and as I think about my father and mother, I can understand more of them. A year ago while I was visiting my folks in Florida, Dad showed me the mailbox on the outside of the house and said to me, "Bob, every day your mother and I go out and look in that mailbox to see if there is word from any of the children." I've thought about that mailbox a lot. It's not much to ask, really, is it—a word from one of the children? But the days and the weeks go by when there isn't any word from me, until I remember the mailbox. How can our parents share their yearnings with us if we aren't in touch? How can we share ours with them?

Abraham Heschel, the elderly Jewish theologian, writes:

> Old age is a major challenge to the inner life . . . old age involves the problem of what to do with privacy . . . there are alleys in the soul where man walks alone, ways that do not lead to society, a world of privacy that shrinks from the public eye. Life comprises not only arable, productive land but also mountains of dreams, an underground of sorrow, towers of yearning . . .[6]

Have you been climbing your dream mountains lately or walking some underground of sorrow or peering out from towers of yearning? Heschel suggests that old age be regarded as a time not for trivial hobbies or entertainments, but for inner growth. He insists that these may be formative years where we seek the insights that we missed along the way. We may seek the wisdom that we ignored and see through the inbred self-deceptions to deeper understanding and compassion for people we don't have to compete with any longer. Have you been growing lately like that?

Heschel puts it finally and beautifully:

> Wisdom is the substance upon which the inner security of the old will forever depend. But the attainment of wisdom is the work of a lifetime. Old men need a vision, not only recreation. Old men need a dream, not only a memory. It

takes three things to attain a sense of significant being: God, a Soul, and a Moment. And the three are always here. Just to be is a blessing. Just to live is holy.[7]

God is in your yearning and in mine. Somehow he embraces us with his love even when we are far apart, and even now he is weaving our separate strands together, though unknown to us, into a tapestry of such rare beauty as we can scarcely imagine.

A young woman shares a beautiful tapestry of yearning:

Ten years ago I received a scrawled, almost illegible letter from an old lady known to me only as my "California Grand-mother." The letter contained this poem:

> Father Time is telling me every day
> the home I live in is wearing away.
> The building is old and for the days that remain
> to seek to repair it would be quite in vain.
> So I'm getting ready to move . . .

One day soon afterward I discovered my grandmother had moved when I received all the letters and photos I had sent her through the years. They were carefully arranged in a red leather case with handwritten instructions on the outside to send the contents back to me. That afternoon I sat with numerous pieces of paper covering my knees: birthday greet-ings wiggily sketched by a five-year-old; crayoned hearts for Valentine Day; my first school picture; long letters from a thirteen-year-old pouring out problems too private for anyone closer to home. As I looked at my life through her eyes, it was an eerie, solemn moment. Beyond the sadness of her death and the nostalgia of my own memories, I suddenly realized that in preparation for her leave-taking, my grand-mother had arranged to send her part of my life back to me; she was giving me back all she loved about me, only better because she was now part of it. And I know that in some inexplicable way, marked by the deepest sadness, the greatest joy, and a bundle of old letters, I have been made a new person through the gift I received from her—a gift freely given, unexpectedly received, made real through life and sanctified forever by death. [8]

What are the distance and depth of *your* yearning?

He Appeared
Also to Me

ONE Good Friday evening I was walking into Burkhart Chapel, a prayer chapel of our church, when I became aware of a young man walking by my side. He said that he had wanted to talk to me for some time, but just never had. So we began to talk. He said to me, "I can't accept Christ. I want to, but I just have no personal, mystical experience of Jesus. Do you?"

By that time we were in the chapel and seated together and I was thinking. I said to him, "No, I don't, either. I wish I did. I envy people who have that mystical one-to-one experience with Jesus. He is most real to me like now, like between us when we are talking together or when there are two or three people gathered together in his name, and there come moments when you understand something that you didn't understand before. You see the light in someone else's eyes. You communicate and you are together. You know that you love each other. Something beautiful is there that wasn't there a moment ago. You know it is real; you know it is his spirit."

We agreed to talk further in the days ahead, and I left. The next morning I came back to the church early and I stopped in the chapel. There was that young man up in front of the altar. He came down the aisle to greet me and I asked him, "Have you been here long?" He said, "Since I saw you last night." Then he showed me a poem he had written during the night, and he left. I began to read the poem:

> Jesus, I don't know you
> at least by a name . . .
> though I think I saw you
> in the springtime rain . . .

As I stood there and read his poem, I realized that Jesus had appeared to me in the face and faith of that young man, calling me to something fresh and new, calling something out of me that wasn't there before. Jesus took me by surprise that Friday night in Burkhart Chapel.

Jesus took Paul by surprise on the road to Damascus. Paul was on his way to arrest Christians in that city when it happened! A shaking realization of a presence burning into his being—the presence, the person of Jesus calling Paul to something new, incredible but real.

Years later, without trying to describe it in detail, Paul reported that experience to the congregation in Corinth in what is our earliest documentary record or report of the resurrection of Jesus. In this letter, he said that Christ "appeared to Cephas [Peter], then to the twelve. Then he appeared to more than five hundred brethren at one time. . . . Then he appeared to James, then to all the apostles. Last of all . . . he appeared also to me." [1]

He appeared also to me! Those five words underline the nature and the meaning of the resurrection event. The earliest New Testament tradition speaks not of an empty tomb (those stories in the Gospels come later) but of appearances of the risen Jesus. Paul uses the same verb *appeared* to describe his own encounter with the risen Christ as he used to describe the encounters the first disciples had with Jesus. This indicates that Paul felt his own experience, which was clearly an encounter not with a physical body but a personal, spiritual presence, to be equally as valid and authentic as that of the disciples. Perhaps this also indicates he believed that their experiences of the risen Jesus and his own were of a similar order, nature, manner, mode. (Paul did not believe in the resurrection of the corpse of Jesus. He put it: "Flesh and blood cannot inherit the kingdom of God . . .")[2]

Easter has not to do with what happened to the corpse of Jesus but what happened in the life of Paul and the other disciples, and what happens in you and me. Easter is not magic, but miracle; not chemistry, but mystery. Easter happens to you and me whenever Jesus takes us by surprise, in some moment of awakening, causing doors that were locked tight to swing open. There is a moment of realization, of looking in the eyes and knowing, "I am loved, I love you, it is possible, a new future is being born."

He appeared also to me in the home of a friend a few weeks ago. A young man in our congregation called me at nine o'clock on a Sunday night and said, "Bob, my dad is here, and some friends. What are you doing? Can you come out and see us and talk?"

I dropped what I was doing, got into the car, and drove out.

A year and a half ago the father of that man had been in church one Sunday morning and something I said in the sermon had offended him, and he had not been back since. His son and I had been waiting, hoping for some time when his father and I might meet face to face and talk. Here it was. I reached the house and went in. Around the fire, on cushions, were the friends of this young man. On the edge of the fireplace was his father, whose face I liked immediately—open, honest, frank, straightforward, clear of eye. We had a little food and a little drink and a little conversation. And we discovered we had many things in common, with respect for some things we saw differently. But what happened, what we all felt there, was that whatever the differences, we were together. We were coming together. The time came to go. We shook hands warmly and moved toward the door. Then just in front of the door, it seemed that we wanted to pray. So we gathered around, with arms around one another, and we prayed. Easter happened to us that night. Jesus took us by surprise in the vestibule of that house.

He appeared to me also in the experience of a woman of our congregation at Camp Akita recently. Let her describe it in her own words:

In the darkened camp lodge at Akita, I sat in a circle of some thirty young people and a few adults. Before us was an altar we had built, surrounded by dozens of twinkling little candles. We had gathered for worship at the end of a weekend retreat together. . . . My friends knew that I had received word early that evening that my mother lay critically ill, and that it was a difficult time for me. . . . Near the end of the worship, a very sensitive and rather shy young man with a guitar introduced a hymn called "Free at Last." Although it was more timely than he knew, somehow he must have

felt the need to allow for my feelings, for he turned to me
and said, "This might not be the best song for right now, but
maybe I can sing another song for you later." I thanked him
with a tight throat and listened hard as the music filtered
softly around the room. . . . After the service I was enfolded
by various expressions of caring, some with words, some with
eyes, and some with warm arms. Later in the evening, I
realized I was being sung to once again. That same young
man with a guitar in hand was indeed playing "another song."
At first I smiled and continued visiting, but then I really
heard what he was playing—"Sometimes I feel like a motherless child, a long way from home." How could he have
known that by dawn I would be motherless and seven hundred miles from my home? As I flew home to say good-by
to my mother and to be with my father, I carried with me
the affirmation and love of a roomful of beautiful people, and
through the pain of those next few days came the confidence
I never thought I'd have . . . to say to those supporting me
. . . "It's all right; it's OK" . . . and to myself, "This is the day
the Lord has made. Let us be glad and rejoice in it." [3]

Jesus appeared to that woman in the presence of death to
affirm life and love, and in the midst of sorrow to start a small
song of joy.

He appeared also to me in a movie called *The Last Picture Show*, a poignant view of life in a small Texas town.
The town is boring. People feel as though their options are
closing off. They yearn for something or someone more.
There is much human unfulfillment in the movie, but also
little oases of human warmth and understanding. A middle-
aged woman talks to a young man about a man they both
loved called Sam the Lion. Sam had died. He was a generous,
compassionate, and courageous man. The woman had been
married to someone else, but she loved Sam in a special way.
She said to this young man, "You know, it's a shame to meet

only one man in your life who knows what you are worth."

I have pondered that comment. Maybe you are lucky if you have even one person who knows what you are worth. It is something to have one person who lets you know how beautiful you are in his eyes, who helps you discover riches that you didn't even know were there, who helps you discover the dimensions of your own being so that you can really believe how precious, how valuable, how full of wonder you are.

Do you know how much you are worth? Do you have one person who knows how much you are worth?

He appeared also to me in the face of a friend in a restaurant not long ago. He said to me, "I am not afraid of the word *cancer*; I am not afraid of the word *death*. I *am* concerned about possible loss of vitality or change in personality. How do I meet it like a man?" Well, he is meeting it like the tremendous man that he is. He is making plans. He is living with confidence and courage to face whatever comes. He is an Easter man. I admire him; I love him.

He appeared also to me in a hospital room this week in the face of a man who has been seriously ill. He pointed to a vase with a long-stemmed rose in it and told me that someone from the church had brought it to him. Then he said quietly to me, "There is a great message in that rose. It says a lot." It said a lot to him of the love of God and his friends in the church. He was not alone, but his friends were with him and the spirit of Jesus was in his room.

He appeared also to me weeks ago in an early Valentine card that someone sent to me. It ended with the words, "You don't have to be infallible to be loved." How beautiful to know that and be reminded of it and to know that someone thinks so. To know that you don't have to be without warts, sins, mistakes, or whatever to be lovable, loved—that somehow you are worth so much that it is worth it, whatever happens. You are so valuable, so precious that nothing can destroy that value, that worth, because the love of Jesus among us is so strong and warm that it can embrace anything and anyone.

He appeared also to me and to our congregation on Maundy Thursday one year when a gift was presented by one of our prisoner friends. This prisoner had been participating in the life of our church for several months, and had recently been a member of one of our groups in Practical Christianity. Our church had come to mean a lot to this man and he presented to us a gift that he had made himself. He is a leather worker and had made in leather a representation of Leonardo da Vinci's "Last Supper." It is a beautiful thing that took many, many hours of work and many hard-earned dollars as well. He gave that gift to us because among us he experienced his own human worth.

He appeared also to me in the faces of some of the members of our church gathered around a table at a restaurant downtown recently. In the midst of ordering and eating mushroom burgers and roquefort burgers and chef salads and so on, people began to share what was happening to them, where they were. All of a sudden a woman there blurted out, "But I am lost. I can't find what I need anywhere, not even at church. I don't know what to do or where to turn." Well, it was as if she had pulled the corks out of our bottles. All the feelings poured out, and all the people began to share where they were and what was happening to them. There were great differences in perspectives, reflecting the nature of our congregation, but people shared, listened, and learned, and began to understand one another. Despite the differences of perspective, once again, that beautiful thing began to happen. We knew that we cared about one another, that somehow we belonged to each other. When we were through, someone offered a prayer for us, and as we left there were expressions of respect and affection. The next day a Thank-U-Gram came from that lost woman with the words, "Thank you, thank you," and three exclamation points. Thank you, Jesus, for taking us by surprise at that restaurant and bringing us together.

He has appeared to you and to me lately, hasn't he, in many ways—a tear, a prayer, a fragment of a melody? He appeared also to Loren Eiseley, an anthropologist, in an experience of resurrection joy, which is a kind of parable of Easter for us. Eiseley was on an expedition to capture some birds to buy for a zoo. He came to an old cabin that had not been occupied for years. He pushed the door of it open. There were holes in the roof where birds had come in to roost in the rafters. He put a ladder against one of the beams. With a flashlight to blind the birds, he crept up until head and arms were over the shelf. Then he flicked on the light, his hand descending on a bird. There was a metallic cry, a beating of feathers, and then a second bird sunk his beak into his hand that held the first one. In the scuffle, the first one got loose, and Eiseley wound up with a lacerated thumb but with a firm grasp on the bird that had done it. It was a fine sparrow hawk in the prime of life. Eiseley was disappointed not to get the hawk's mate, but he took the one he had, put it in a box, and laid it away for the evening.

The next morning he brought the box outside, put it on the grass, and prepared to make a cage for the bird. He looked up and all around to see if there was any sign of the other young sparrow hawk, but evidently she had gone. On an impulse, Eiseley took the bird out of the box.

He lay limp in my grasp and I could feel his heart pound under the feathers, but he only looked beyond me and up. I saw him look that last look away beyond me into a sky so full of light that I could not follow his gaze. . . . I suppose I must have had an idea then of what I was going to do, but I never let it come to consciousness. I just reached over and laid the hawk on the grass. He lay there a long minute without hope, unmoving, his eyes still fixed on that blue vault above him. It must have been that he was already so far away in heart that he never felt the release from my hand. He never even stood. He just lay with his breast against the grass. In the next second after that long minute he was gone. Like a flicker of light he had vanished with my eyes full on him. . . . For another long moment there was silence. I could not see him. The light was too intense. Then from far up somewhere a cry came ringing down. . . . It was not the cry of the hawk I had captured; for, by shifting my position against the sun, I was now seeing further up. Straight out of the sun's eye, where she must have been soaring restlessly above us for untold hours, hurtled his mate. . . . I saw them both now. He was rising to meet her. . . . And from far up, ringing from peak to peak of the summits over us, came a cry of such unutterable and ecstatic joy that it sounds down across the years and tingles among the cups on my quiet breakfast table.[4]

Has He appeared to you lately?

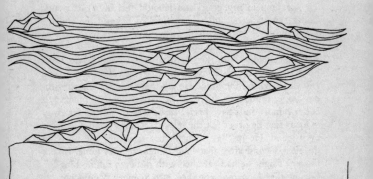

Trust the Process

TRUST THE process? That is one of the hardest things for me to do. I want to control the process, if possible, or at least manage it. But trust it? Let it go its own way, whatever that may be? Yield myself up to the shift and turn of events? It almost seems irresponsible and more than a little scary. Maybe you have trouble trusting the process, too. Let's explore it together and see where the process of exploration may take us.

For openers, when we don't trust the process, we try to control the future in one way or another. We use different styles of trying to control the future which are indigenous to our own being and temperament. There is *the bureaucratic style* of controlling the future in which we become the logical thinker, laying out the future in graphs and statistics, organizing committees and task forces, squeezing the future dry of its creative and joyous juices and hanging on to the husk of our analysis even as life overflows our tidy technology. Or there is *the seductive style* of controlling the future in which we become a smiling seducer, wittingly or unwittingly charming those about us with unceasing good will, smiling our way past real conflict and opposition, working our own purposes through geniality. Or there is *the paranoid style* of controlling the future, in which we become a fearful list-maker of what will happen today, tomorrow, next year, afraid to leave any eventuality unanticipated. We fence in the future so as to protect ourselves against any uncertainty and thus any spontaneity. Or there is the *gangbusters* style of controlling the future, the aggressive battler, in which we take the future by the scruff of the neck and shake it. It is a "zap-them-before-they-zap-you" approach, which works somewhat better in a football game than it does in a family or a university or a corporation or a city. Then there is *the dependent style* of controlling the future in which we become the friendly helper and facilitator. We fill other people's needs carefully and thus get them in our debt so that we can say in one way or another to them, "After all I've done for you—" Husbands and wives, parents and children work this as a way of controlling the future.

Can we see ourselves in one or more of these styles?

Paul was speaking to people like you and me when he said to the congregation at Philippi, "Have no anxiety about anything, but in everything . . . let your requests be made known to God. And the peace of God . . . will keep your hearts and your minds in Christ Jesus." [1] Have no anxiety about *anything*, in *everything* trust God. How is it possible for us to trust the process of our lives like that? What would it feel like and look like?

I got some insight into that question one day this summer when Nancy, our twelve-year-old, and Bobby, our six-year-old, and I climbed into a canoe to go down the Crystal River in Michigan. It is a shallow, narrow stream that winds and undulates through woods and meadows, shoots through a couple of culverts, and eventually goes into Lake Michigan. It had been a while since I had negotiated a fast-flowing river like that in a canoe, so for the first few minutes as the current caught us and whipped us around, I found myself shouting at Nancy, "Paddle on the right side, no, on the left—" and "Bobby, quit trying to reach for that branch. Sit down or we are going to turn over!" We were trying to maneuver the canoe around this rock and past that branch until finally I let the canoe take its own head and follow the current of the stream. I found that with a little stroke here and a little push there, a bit of finesse and timing, it was possible to trust the process of that river.

If we think of our lives like the flow of a river, we realize there is a timing, a tide in our being and in our relationships. There is a flow and a movement of the spirit, the natural unfolding of the initiatives of people, and the constellation of events. We discover again and again that no matter how hard we try to cover for every possible contingency, the plans of mice and men—and ours—can go astray, can go awry. The coming future with its novelty and spontaneity outwits us always with its strange newness and unpredictable happenings, so that we need a deep confidence and flexibility of spirit enabling us to trust the process. We need, in a few words, *to go with the flow* and *to use a light touch*.

What does it mean to go with the flow? When we realized, in the canoe, that the flow of the river was not against us, but for us, then it was possible for us to go with the flow of the river, in the confidence that our own purpose could best be served by cooperating with the direction and movement of that current. When we come really to believe deep down that the flow of our lives, the underlying currents that are moving in us and about us, are not against us but are for us, that the spirit of God is literally in the flux and movement of our lives, then it becomes possible for us to go with the flow of our lives in the confidence that God is with us literally in everything. Gradually we may be able to accept the provisional character of the universe and of our lives with both its meaning of contingency and generosity.

The other night Bobby cried out in his sleep. When I went into his room, I found he had fallen out of the bed onto the floor and was crying. He mumbled something about a bad dream. I picked him up, put him back in bed, and said to him, "Don't be afraid, you're OK, everything is all right." When we say that to our children or to one another, we do not lie, though we know we cannot guarantee safety for any of those we love throughout life. We are making a faith statement about the universe and its ultimate power when we say to one another, "Don't be afraid, you're OK, everything is all right. No matter what happens to you, no matter what can happen to you, no matter what you may be or do, it's OK, don't be afraid, everything is all right."

Erik Erikson, psychoanalyst, says that the development of this primal trust in the first year of a child's life is absolutely necessary for that child to grow into healthy childhood. He must sense through his mother primarily, and then through other people, that there is a hallowed presence near him which can be depended upon, which cares for him, in whose everlasting arms he is OK, and that everything is all right.

Sometimes it is possible to sense that hallowed presence, to know even in the midst of tragedy and death that somehow it is ок, everything is all right. Recently I was in the home of a family of our congregation whose father lay dying on his bed. He had known for some months that he had a terminal illness, as the family had known. The family had begun to gather from around the country in anticipation of his death coming very soon. But that afternoon we gathered around his bedside and talked a bit, and he smiled, unable to speak words very clearly. Then, because the Twenty-Third Psalm had long been a favorite of his and he had repeated it in recent days, we joined hands around his bedside and together repeated it. His mouth, his lips, moved a little bit but words did not come out until the end of the psalm, when he said very clearly, "Amen." There was a sense that I felt—and I think the others did, too— that in the midst of death this man was ок, that everything was really, finally, all right, and that he knew it.

To go with the flow of your life is to live without a map— to be vulnerable to having your mind and your plans changed, your heart broken, your dreams fulfilled. It is to trust that God is in the rapids of change as well as in the rocks of continuity. It is being able to stop digging your heels in against the tide of tomorrow. It's to be forever on your way to keeping your tryst with tomorrow. The poet Roethke wrote a little line which I love: "I learn by going where I have to go." [2] Go with the flow then, and use the light touch.

Trusting the process is a deeper thing than just letting it be. It is not a fatalistic *che sarà, sarà* (whatever will be, will be). It includes the responsibility of choice, of action, of response, *of using a light touch*, exercising a suppleness of spirit in which we respond to the nudgings and promptings of grace moment by moment, day by day, in a kind of love-making with life. Surely there are times when a heavy hand is necessary, when you have to paddle like crazy or jab away at the shore to get around and go downstream. Or, to make it, there are other times when you have a clear clean shot and you can just sail down that river and lift up your paddle and say, "Look, Lord, no hands, no hands!" But most of the time in our relationships it is a matter of using a light touch, a deft stroke here and a decisive twist or a flick of the wrist there that brings you into that rippling turn around the beautiful shoreline and on down the river. Sensitivity and finesse, timing, love-making, responding to the wooing signals of human hope and heartache.

The heartache is sometimes hard for us. Paul urges us to offer up everything that happens to us with thanksgiving. *Everything* with *thanksgiving*! Is it possible for us to offer up even our hurts, our heartaches, our betrayals, our sorrows, with thanksgiving? Somewhere Nietzsche says, "We must love our wounds." I'm not sure what all of that means, but I think a part of what it means is that my wounds are part of the new being that I am becoming, yet I can, because of God, accept every dimension of myself, the dark side as well as the light side. Because of God, I can accept everything that happens to me in the knowledge that somehow God has power to redeem it and make it some way all right. I can "trust God and sin on bravely" in the knowledge that my hope lies not in my virtue but in his grace, and that because he is in everything, we can trust the process and use a light touch to facilitate the future.

Recently I had a conversation with a friend. Though I had a very specific intention as to the outcome of that conversation, by the end of it we had moved in an entirely different and unanticipated direction. I realized later that he had used a light touch with me, that in a very kindly way he had opened up other options for me to consider, nudging me to think of this and look at that, leaving me elbow room and therefore leaving God elbow room.

A letter came to some parents of our congregation from one of their children. This was a young woman with whom, over a period of many years, there had been long times of poor communication, lots of heartaches and mistakes, and terrible frustration and uncertainty. As parents, they had gone through every stage of trying to figure out some way to know what to do and what not to do; and finally they didn't know what to do. Kids feel the same way sometimes about their parents, but this young woman began to find herself, took a trip by herself, met another girl and they traveled together. She wrote a beautiful letter to her folks with a P.S. on it:

. . . As we rounded the bend in one mountain we came upon a sudden blue lake, with ranges of pyramid pines stretching for miles behind. I was really taken aback. There was one young man who really expressed how I felt. He had pulled his car over to the side of the road and had gotten out his trumpet and was blowing his heartfelt melody to the gods. A really good thanksgiving!"

And then in big letters she had written "I love you! Thank you for my life and my love of it!"

Go with the flow, use a light touch, and the peace of God will guide your heart and mind, no matter how far out on the river you get away from your home base. We are like blind men on a river—like that really blind man, Robert Russell, who describes so beautifully in the book *To Catch an Angel* what it was like living on an island in the river and how he arranged to go out on that river, blind, by himself. He says:

So that I can go out by myself whenever I please, I have run a wire down to the end of the dock, where I have mounted a large electric bell. Before I go down to the dock, I plug the line into an outlet in the house. A timing device permits the bell to ring only once every thirty seconds. If I row too far upwind to be able to hear the bell, I can still fish without anxiety because I can always drift downwind and then I am again in touch with my base.

And a man needs a base to quest from, and he needs the sense that, however far he has strayed, return is still possible. Confidence that he has such a base is all that gives him the courage to reach past the edges of the familiar. . . . The river lies before me, a constant invitation, a constant challenge, and my bell is the thread of sound along which I return.

To a quiet base.[3]

Go with the flow of the river, use a light touch to negotiate your way, and trust the process.

NOTES

CHAPTER 1

1. Richard L. Rubenstein, *After Auschwitz* (Indianapolis: Bobbs-Merrill, 1966), chapter 2.
2. Loren Eiseley, *The Unexpected Universe* (New York: Harcourt, Brace and World, 1969), p. 55.
3. Bedouin guide story from Samuel Terrien, *Job: Poet of Existence* (Indianapolis: Bobbs-Merrill, 1957), p. 165.
4. James Baldwin, *Another Country* (New York: Dial Press, 1962), pp. 8–9.

CHAPTER 2

1. Alexander Solzhenitsyn, *The First Circle*, tr. Thomas P. Whitney (New York: Harper & Row, 1968), p. 139.
2. Ibid.
3. 2 Cor. 4:7–10, RSV.
4. Solzhenitsyn, *The First Circle*, p. 140.
5. Ibid., p. 139.
6. 2 Cor. 4:16–18, NEB.
7. Gay Talese, *The Kingdom and the Power* (New York: World Publishing Co., 1969), p. 13.
8. Chester Bowles, *Ambassador's Report* (New York: Harper and Brothers, 1954), p. 74.

CHAPTER 3

1. Isa. 40:27, RSV.
2. Isa. 40:28–31, RSV.
3. *King Lear*, in *The Tragedies of Shakespeare* (New York: Random House, Modern Library), act 2, sc. 5, p. 732.
4. Ibid., act 4, sc. 7, p. 771.
5. Ibid., act 5, sc. 3, p. 776.
6. Fyodor Dostoyevsky, *The Brothers Karamazov* (New York: Random House, Modern Library), p. 126.

7. Albert Camus, *The Plague* (New York: Random House, Modern Library, 1948), p. 278.

CHAPTER 4

1. Norman Podhoretz, *Making It* (New York: Random House, 1967), p. xi.
2. Mark 10:35–37, NEB.
3. Podhoretz, p. 96.
4. Ibid., p. 354.
5. Mark 10:42–45, NEB.

CHAPTER 5

1. Matt. 8:20, RSV.
2. Rainer Maria Rilke, *Letters to a Young Poet* (New York: Norton, 1954), pp. 29–30.

CHAPTER 6

1. Lorraine Hansberry, *The Sign in Sidney Brustein's Window* (New York: New American Library, Signet Books), act 2, sc. 1, p. 256.
2. Phil. 4:11–13, RSV.
3. Kenneth Clark, *Civilisation* (New York: Harper & Row, 1969), p. 4.

CHAPTER 7

1. Pennsylvania Law Enforcement Journal, reprinted in Robert Raines, ed., *Creative Brooding* (New York: Macmillan, 1966), pp. 81–82.
2. Rom. 8:39, NEB.
3. Dietrich Bonhoeffer, *Letters and Papers from Prison* (London: SCM Press Ltd., 1953), pp. 85, 91.
4. Letter written by Judy Fountain after the birth of her daughter, Jennifer.

Notes

CHAPTER 8

1. New York *Times* editorial, "The Continuity," December, 1971. © 1971 by The New York Times Company. Reprinted by permission.
2. Rev. 21:1–5, NEB.
3. William Blake, "Auguries of Innocence."
4. Anais Nin, in John Pearson, *Kiss the Joy As It Flies* (Berkeley, Calif.: The Bookworks, 1971), unnumbered pages 12, 47. I would like especially to acknowledge this lovely book as the place I first came in contact with the Blake quote, which has been an inspiration in my personal life and in my ministry.
5. Poem sent to author.

CHAPTER 9

1. Solzhenitsyn, *The First Circle*, p. 34.
2. Alexander Solzhenitsyn, *Cancer Ward* (New York: Grosset & Dunlap, Bantam Books, 1969), p. 266.
3. Solzhenitsyn, *The First Circle*, p. 374.
4. Viktor Frankl, *Man's Search for Meaning* (New York: Simon & Schuster, Pocket Books, 1973), p. 104.
5. N. Richard Nash, *The Rainmaker* (New York: Grosset & Dunlap, Bantam Books, 1957), act 3, p. 102.

CHAPTER 10

1. Mark 5:9, TEV.
2. Melvin Maddocks, "Look Back on Anger," *Time*, August 16, 1971, p. 40. Reprinted by permission from *Time*, The Weekly Newsmagazine; Copyright 1971 Time Inc. All rights reserved.
3. Sam Keen, *To a Dancing God* (New York: Harper & Row, 1970), pp. 117-10. Copyright © 1970 by Sam Keen. By permission of Harper & Row, Publishers, Inc.
4. Ibid., pp. 119–20.

CHAPTER 11

1. Harper Lee, *To Kill a Mockingbird* (Philadelphia: J. B. Lippincott, 1960), p. 105.

2. Gen. 32:24, RSV.
3. Chaim Potok, *My Name Is Asher Lev* (New York: Alfred A. Knopf, 1972), p. 212.
4. Gen. 32:26–28, RSV.
5. John Updike, *Rabbit Redux* (New York: Alfred A. Knopf, 1971), p. 261.
6. Rilke, *Letters to a Young Poet*, pp. 67-68.
7. Updike, *Rabbit Redux*, p. 78.
8. Israel Shenker, "What It's Like to Be 67 and Blind," *New York Times*, February 7, 1971. © 1971 by The New York Times Company. Reprinted by permission.

CHAPTER 12

1. Phil. 1:7–8, RSV.
2. "The Command Generation," in Modern Living, *Time*, July 29, 1966, p. 51.
3. Kenneth J. Gergen, "Multiple Identity—The Healthy, Happy Human Being Wears Many Masks," *Psychology Today*, May 1972, p. 31.
4. Walt Whitman, "Song of Myself," in *Leaves of Grass*.
5. Georges Simenon, *When I Was Old* (New York: Harcourt Brace Jovanovich, 1970), pp. 9, 190.
6. Abraham Heschel, "To Grow in Wisdom," *The Christian Ministry*, March 1971, p. 32.
7. Ibid., p. 37.
8. Letter written by Joan Hemenway for Lenten publication of First United Methodist Church of Germantown, Philadelphia, Pa.

CHAPTER 13

1. 1 Cor. 15:5–8, RSV.
2. 1 Cor. 15:50, RSV.
3. Devotion presented by Cindy Swearingen to Women's Guild, First Community Church, Columbus, Ohio.

4. Loren Eiseley, *The Immense Journey* (New York: Random House, 1957), pp. 188–193.

CHAPTER 14

1. Phil. 4:6–7, RSV.
2. Theodore Roethke, *Words for the Wind* (Bloomington: Indiana University Press, 1961), "The Waking," p. 124.
3. Robert Russell, *To Catch an Angel* (New York: Vanguard Press, 1962), pp. 313–14.